TRAVELLER

CUBA

By
MARTIN HASTINGS

Written by Martin Hastings, updated by Claire Boobbyer
Original photography by John Harden, update photography by
Claire Boobbyer

Published by Thomas Cook Publishing
A division of Thomas Cook Tour Operations Limited.
Company registration no. 1450464 England
The Thomas Cook Business Park, Unit 9, Coningsby Road,
Peterborough PE3 8SB, United Kingdom
E-mail: books@thomascook.com, Tel: + 44 (0) 1733 416477
www.thomascookpublishing.com

Produced by Cambridge Publishing Management Limited
Burr Elm Court, Main Street, Caldecote CB23 7NU

ISBN: 978-1-84157-950-4

© 2004, 2006 Thomas Cook Publishing
This third edition © 2008
Text © Thomas Cook Publishing
Maps © Thomas Cook Publishing

Series Editor: Maisie Fitzpatrick
Production/DTP: Steven Collins

Printed and bound in Italy by: Printer Trento

Cover photography: Front: © Schmid Reinhard/SIME-4Corners Images;
© Pictures Colour Library; ©Pictures Colour Library
Back: © Ripani Massimo/SIME-4Corners Images; © Ian Mckinnell/
Getty Images

The paper used for this book has been independently certified as having
been sourced from well-managed forests and recycled wood or fibre
according to the rules of the Forest Stewardship Council.
This book has been printed and bound in Italy by Printer Trento S.r.l.,
an FSC certified company for printing books on FSC mixed paper in
compliance with the chain of custody and on products labelling standards.

FSC
Mixed Sources
Product group from well-managed
forests and recycled wood or fibre
Cert no. CQ-COC-000012
www.fsc.org
© 1996 Forest Stewardship Council

Contents

KEY TO MAPS

✈ Airport   🏛 Museum

🚩 Church   ✚ Hospital

Railway line   ④ Road number

✉ Post office   ☏ Public telephone

$ Bank   ═══ Motorway

ℹ Information   🚌 Bus station

Introduction

Cuba has come a long way in the last 20 years. The country is transforming itself from an old-fashioned, inefficient and slightly downmarket destination for travellers to one that has attractive facilities, a more robust infrastructure and an attitude to service and efficiency that makes visiting Cuba a pleasurable and exciting experience.

It is not hard to understand why Cuba has become a favourite of travel experts: beautiful white beaches with crystal-clear waters attract package holiday-makers and water sports enthusiasts; Havana is regaining its former splendour, with systematic restoration of the Old City; Cuban music is wildly popular abroad, with many travellers visiting just for the nightlife and salsa dancing; and nature lovers are increasingly drawn to the richness of flora, fauna, unspoilt countryside and the spectacular marine life of the island.

Managing one's expectations is the first challenge that a visitor will have to face when planning a visit. Any number of viewings of *The Buena Vista Social Club*, documentaries about the Cuban Revolution, or listening to Cuban salsa music will not prepare you for the experience of being in Cuba. It is like no country you have ever visited, so do not expect an archetypally Caribbean island or a typical Latin American country, for it is neither.

Many visitors to Cuba tend to come on package holidays, and only ever get to see the all-inclusive beach resort in which they are staying, as well as a day or two in the capital, Havana. This is a great shame, because Cuba has so much more to offer, and visitors just need a small injection of confidence to look beyond the clichés and experience the real Cuba.

There are delightful colonial towns such as Trinidad, tranquil and rich natural habitats such as the Península de Zapata, and there are more beaches and top-notch diving spots than you could imagine. Cuba can cater to many tastes; you just need a bit of planning, an open mind and a thirst for adventure that will reap great rewards in your time on the island.

In these days of globalisation and runaway capitalism, Cuba is one of the few countries in the western hemisphere that has the capacity to challenge one's most ingrained assumptions about governance, money, family, freedom and happiness in general. Its contradictions are many. How can a communist country be so good at attracting foreign package holiday-makers? How can Havana still be so beautiful even after more than 40 years of neglect? How can a country so poor have such a healthy and educated population? How have this country's ideals and culture survived this long on the doorstep of the world's biggest capitalist superpower? The questions will keep coming to you long after you have left the country.

NATIONAL SYMBOLS

The national flower is the butterfly lily (a type of white-coloured jasmine that is exquisitely perfumed), while the national bird is the trogon (a native species whose plumage contains the same colours as the Cuban flag). The royal palm is the national tree and is found in abundance throughout the island.

Like many, you are likely to feel a mixture of perplexity, admiration and warmth for this large, isolated island in the middle of the sun-kissed Caribbean Sea.

The colourful Callejón de Hammel in Centro Habana

The land

Known as the key to the Gulf, Cuba is the largest of the West Indies and one of the largest islands in the world. Shaped rather like a crocodile, it is a long, narrow island in the westernmost part of the insular Caribbean, at the entrance of the Gulf of Mexico.

The island is 1,200km (746 miles) long and reaches 210km (130 miles) at its widest point. The Cuban archipelago comprises an area of 110,992sq km (42,850sq miles) and has more than 300 natural beaches of fine white sand lapped by crystal-clear waters, the most famous being Varadero. Cuba has a wide variety of landscapes, ranging from plains to hilly and mountainous areas. The three most important mountain ranges are Cordillera de Guaniguanico, in the western part of the country, Escambray in the centre, and Sierra Maestra in the east, with Turquino peak, the highest point in the country, at 1,974m (6,476ft) above sea level. The rest of the territory is plain and fertile. There are plenty of caves, some of outstanding beauty, such as Bellamar in Matanzas province.

Most rivers in Cuba are relatively short and the water currents are quite strong. They flow through the mountains, creating beautiful waterfalls such as Salto del Caburní and Agabama

Falls. Cuba's longest river is the Cauto, about 240km (150 miles) long, located in the east. There are also many reservoirs and lakes. In rural areas, lush natural settings make for spectacular scenery, and migratory routes for birdlife can be seen in the countryside. Rural life operates in different ways and confers its own unique characteristics on the Cuban countryside.

Urban areas contain 75 per cent of the population, while the remainder

A *mogote* (limestone outcrop) in western Cuba

lives in the countryside. On the whole, Cuban towns contain a wide mix of architectural styles, although many buildings are run-down. However, in some cities' old quarters, for example Havana or Trinidad, a colonial ambience has been preserved.

Flora and fauna

Cuba's flora and fauna are very rich and diverse. There are more than 300 protected areas that cover approximately 22 per cent of the national territory, and the country has six areas that have been declared Biosphere Reserves by UNESCO: Guanahacabibes Peninsula, Sierra del Rosario and Ciénaga de Zapata National Park in the west; El Caguanes National Park in the centre; and

Baconao Park and Cuchillas del Toa in the east. More than 50 per cent of Cuba's flora is endemic and its variety is illustrated by the fact that Cuba holds 4 per cent of the total flora species on the planet. Most appealing among these are orchids, cacti and the palm tree.

Endemic species are also much in evidence when it comes to amphibians and reptiles. The crocodile, commonly found in crocodile breeding centres in the country, is very characteristic of Cuba. Around 400 species of bird are estimated to exist in Cuba, and the country still preserves rare species like the *zunzuncito* which is the smallest bird in the world, as well as the tiniest frog, a very small bat called *mariposa* (butterfly bat) and a scorpion no longer than 14mm (1/2 inch).

Cuba's provinces and main attractions

History

The recorded history of Cuba begins with the arrival of Christopher Columbus on 28 October 1492. Before this, Cuba is thought to have been inhabited by three Amerindian ethnic groups. The Guanajatabey were gatherers who lived in caves; next came the Siboney who were hunters and fishermen; and lastly the Taíno, who came from present-day Venezuela and were the most advanced of the three groups.

Columbus landed in Cuba during his first voyage of discovery in the New World. He was disappointed not to find gold but was intrigued by the Amerindian practice of puffing at burning rolls of leaves which they called *tabacos*. The island was quickly conquered by the Spanish, mainly due to the relative lack of resistance put up by the Indians, with the exception of chief Hatuey, who was burnt at the stake. Key in this conquest was Diego de Velázquez, who completed the annexation of the island to Spain in 1514, and set up several towns (*villas*), including Havana.

The native Indian population was decimated by a combination of forced labour, cruelty, and European viruses, which they were completely unable to cope with. Because of this, by 1526 the Spanish had started to import slaves from Africa.

Cuba was used by the Spanish as a port of call for ships taking riches from the New World back to Spain, and as a strategic military base for their colonies. By the 16th century, this wealth attracted the attention of pirates, buccaneers and corsairs, the latter sanctioned by Britain, France and the Netherlands. This led to the building of impressive fortifications around the main ports of Cuba, including Havana.

Sugar cane and tobacco began to be cultivated on a large scale and were traded solely with Spain. Havana was briefly occupied by the British in 1762, but they left the following year as a result of the Treaty of Paris, in exchange for Florida. One of the results of this brief occupation was that Cuban landowners began to realise that trading with other countries besides Spain was a more economically attractive proposition.

By the end of the 18th century, Cuba was a plantation society with a Creole aristocracy, Cuban-born people of Spanish descent who soon established a Cuban national identity. Nationalist revolts were put down by the Spanish, but the newly-emerged Creole middle class were determined to gain independence for their country from the Spanish crown.

On 10 October 1868, Carlos Manuel de Céspedes, a Creole landowner, freed his slaves, triggering the first Cuban war of independence. This Ten Years War ended in 1878 with the Convention of Zanjón, which was rejected by some revolutionaries, including the famous General Antonio Maceo, Máximo Gómez and de Céspedes himself. War resumed in 1895, with José Martí, a Cuban intellectual, at the forefront of the struggle. In the meantime, the USA was becoming concerned about the substantial investments that it had been building up in Cuba, especially in the form of sugar plantations and mills. The explosion of the US battleship *Maine* in Havana harbour in February 1898 was the excuse that the USA needed for declaring war on Spain. The US Navy defeated the Spanish fleet and the Treaty of Paris was subsequently signed between the USA and Spain, which ignored Cuban interests. Cuban nationalists realised that they were at last free from their Spanish colonial masters, but were under US military occupation for the next four years, and under US 'supervision' for the next 30 or so years.

Formal independence was granted to Cuba on 20 May 1902, but the new Republic was constrained by the Platt Amendment, passed by US Congress, which enabled the USA to retain its naval bases, including the one in Guantánamo Bay, and reserved the right to intervene in Cuban domestic affairs. Cuba was essentially dependent on the USA for trade, there were huge social inequalities, and the majority of rural people suffered grinding poverty. As a result, resentment against the USA for its political and economic domination of the island was to prove one of the driving forces behind the Cuban Revolution in the 1950s.

From 1924 to 1933 Cuba was ruled by Gerardo Machado, a dictator who oversaw a period of tyranny, political corruption and strikes. Sergeant Fulgencio Batista became a key figure in the ensuing years, heading a revolt of army officers and placing several presidential puppets, before holding power himself in the years 1933–44. A series of presidents followed, but they failed to halt the corruption, political violence and public discontent. On 1 June 1952, Batista staged a military coup, and ruled Cuba with violent repression of mostly student demonstrations, and a disdain for the common Cuban, who became ever poorer. Batista was backed by the Americans, and turned Cuba into a glamorous 'pleasure island', with prostitution, gambling and a sensual tropical life that attracted American businessmen, film stars and mafiosi. It was this state of affairs that was to lead to the Cuban Revolution.

The Cuban Revolution

The importance of the Cuban Revolution in the history of the island cannot be underestimated. It changed everything: not only the political ideology and government of Cuba, but its culture, economy, international relations, national identity and ideals, which have remained virtually unchanged for nearly 50 years.

The Cuban Revolution effectively began with Batista's coup in 1952, which led to the denouncement of his new government by Fidel Castro Ruz, an active student leader. This found support from a large number of ordinary Cubans, but peaceful protests had little effect. Castro and his close associates decided to turn to violent means to achieve their aims, starting with the unsuccessful raid on the Moncada army barracks in Santiago de Cuba. Many were captured and executed, but Castro and several others escaped. Castro's life was saved by the army officer who captured him, who recognised him from their student days and decided not to take him back to Santiago de Cuba to face certain torture and death. Castro and others, including his brother Raúl, were imprisoned on the Isla de la Juventud but only served two years before being granted amnesty. Castro's defence speech during the trial was to become the basis of a reform programme and a summary of his revolutionary thinking, named after the famous last sentence: 'History will absolve me.'

After a period in exile in Mexico, where he met Che Guevara, Castro set up the '26 July Movement' and formed a band of 82 revolutionaries. They sailed on the yacht *Granma* to the southeastern tip of Cuba on 2 December 1956, and, after being surprised by Batista's troops, escaped to the Sierra Maestra mountains. There, they rallied support and trained an army of guerrillas, launching attacks on government troops and taking their supplies and weapons. Popular support was greatly strengthened by the setting up of a guerrilla radio station Radio Rebelde, which was avidly listened to all over the island. The growing numbers of *barbudos* ('bearded men', so called because they all grew beards during their time in the mountains) were joined by a mixture of students, farmers, army deserters and city men recruited by the urban branch of the 'Movimiento 26 de Julio'.

The fighting reached its peak in 1958 when two columns of guerrillas marched through the island, one led by Che Guevara and Camilo Cienfuegos which headed west to the centre of the island, and the other led by Raúl Castro which headed towards Guantánamo. The Battle of Santa Clara was decisive: Che Guevara's troops overcame government forces against overwhelming odds, and captured a troop train laden with supplies and armaments. As a result,

Batista fled Cuba on 31 December 1958, and victory was declared for the revolution. On 1 January 1959, Che Guevara and Camilo Cienfuegos entered Havana in triumph, while Castro did the same in Santiago de Cuba.

Manuel Urrutia was initially elected president upon Batista's escape, but by 16 February Fidel Castro was persuaded to take office after initially refusing, and was elected prime minister.

Fidel Castro and his troops, 1956

Economic isolation

The Cuban Revolution, which took control of the island in 1959, was the catalyst for hostility from the USA, leading to economic sanctions. These have had a profound effect on the economy of Cuba.

From 1960 onwards, Fidel Castro led Cuba down the path to socialism in the face of huge pressure from the USA, which only hardened the leftward leanings of the regime. All foreign banks, sugar and oil refineries, foreign-owned companies and private property were nationalised. The USA lost its substantial economic assets, and the US mafia lost its money-laundering operations, including gambling, prostitution, hotels and nightclubs. Following the unsuccessful Bay of Pigs invasion in 1961, Fidel Castro declared that Cuba was socialist, and established mutual benefit treaties and strong relations with the USSR, China and North Korea. The USA responded by severing diplomatic relations with Cuba and installing a full trade embargo.

The effect soon began to be felt, with rationing imposed in March 1962 which continues even today. Cuba became more economically dependent on the USSR, relying on favourable trade terms for oil, and receiving millions in economic aid, machinery and technicians, equivalent to 25 per cent of Cuba's wealth. By the 1980s, living standards for Cubans still had not improved and further austerity was experienced with the Latin American debt crisis.

With the collapse of the communist system in the USSR by the early 1990s, Castro realised the necessity of gaining foreign earnings in the face of the cessation of aid and economic assistance from the USSR. A programme of economic liberalisation ensued, with farmers' markets being allowed to operate.

Tourism has become a priority: there has been massive foreign investment, particularly from Canadian, Spanish and other European corporations, especially along the Varadero coast, in order to attract package holiday-makers. As a result, visitor numbers are forecast to rise from 2 million in 2002 to 7 million in 2010.

One growing social problem as a result of Cuba's economic isolation is the widening income gap between those who earn Cuban Convertible Pesos (CUC) in the tourist industry and the majority who don't. Because the majority of the population earn

Cuban pesos (*moneda nacional*), and most consumer goods are sold in CUCs, this makes many products way out of reach of most ordinary Cubans. As a result, some Cubans will do practically anything to earn CUCs from tourists.

To give an example of the current rationing system, the average Cuban adult will be allowed to buy five eggs per month, 3kg (6.5lb) of rice, and various quantities of other produce including beans, sugar and salt. Cubans have ration books which allow them to buy these amounts at low national prices. Anything over and above this is available in private markets at much higher prices, in CUCs.

Cuba is also a world leader in research and exports in the pharmaceutical and biotechnological industries. Other industries include those for construction materials, fishing, nickel mining (the country holds the largest open-face reserves in the world), copper, magnesium and refractory chrome.

Cuba is diversifying its economy, especially in agriculture, in order to reduce its dependence on imported foreign food. The gradual move to a more unstructured economy that allows private enterprise will inevitably lead to 'growing pains' as the country adapts. In the meantime, however, there is no sign that the US trade embargo will be relaxed. This is mainly because of the importance of Florida, and especially Miami, to any US presidential candidate, a state with a large and vocal anti-Castro, Cuban émigré population, which is vehemently opposed to the relaxation of the trade embargo.

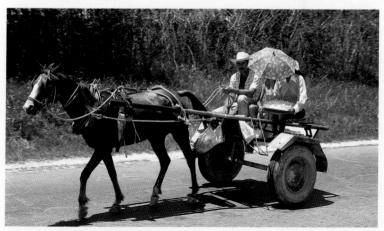

A horse-drawn cart fitted with lorry wheels

History timeline

1492 Cuba discovered by Christopher Colombus (Cristóbal Colón in Spanish) on his first voyage. He claims the island for Spain.

1514 The annexation of Cuba is completed by the Spanish under Diego de Velázquez.

1519 The city of San Cristóbal de La Habana is founded on the site of present-day Havana.

1526 The Spanish begin the importation of slaves from Africa.

1555 Havana is sacked by the Frenchman Jacques de Sores, leading to extensive fortifications at Cuban ports. Havana is established as the gathering point of all Spanish colonial fleets.

1762 British forces occupy Havana and leave the following year after the Treaty of Paris.

1793 Commerce with the USA is formally established although unofficial links are already in place.

1820 The Spanish constitutional regime is re-established, leading to pro-independence pressures, led by priest Félix Varela.

1837 The first railway in Cuba, the third in the world, is built to support the booming sugar industry.

1868 Carlos Manuel de Céspedes, a Creole landowner, frees his slaves, triggering the first Cuban war of independence (or the Ten Years War).

1878 The Ten Years War ends with the Convention of Zanjón. This is rejected by some revolutionaries, including General Antonio Maceo, and is known as the protest of Baraguá.

1880 Slavery is formally abolished, although its practice only ceases six years later.

1892 The Cuban Revolutionary Party is founded by José Martí as part of the struggle for independence.

1895	The last War of Independence against Spanish colonial rule begins, and José Martí dies in combat.
1896	Antonio Maceo dies fighting the Spanish.
1898	The explosion of the US battleship *Maine* in Havana harbour leads to American intervention in the War of Independence, and the defeat of the Spanish navy.
1902	Cuba achieves independence but is supervised by the USA as a neo-colonial republic.
1925	The Communist Party of Cuba is founded by Carlos Baliño.
1933	US-backed dictator Gerardo Machado forced to resign after ten years in power.
1940	A democratic and liberal constitution put into force.
1952	Army general Fulgencio Batista stages a military coup and suspends the constitution.
1953	Revolutionaries headed by Fidel Castro stage a failed assault on the Moncada Garrison.

1956	Castro, Che Guevara and 82 revolutionaries resume the struggle.
1959	The Revolution triumphs after Batista flees Cuba.
1961	US-backed Cuban exiles launch a failed invasion at the Bay of Pigs.
1962	The USSR removes its missiles from Cuban soil.
1976	The Constitution of the Republic of Cuba put into effect with elections to the National Assembly.
1982	Old Havana declared a UNESCO World Heritage Site.
1998	Pope John Paul II visits.
2002	US naval base at Guantánamo Bay used to intern al-Qaeda and Taliban prisoners.
2005	Cuba is hit by a series of very damaging hurricanes.
2006	Fidel Castro falls ill. His brother Raúl takes over his duties.
Feb 2008	Fidel announces his retirement. National Assembly elects Raúl president.

Politics

Although the Castro regime has been severe and liable to periodic crackdowns on dissidents, it is still popular and there is a tangible sense of national pride among the population. Much of this is due to the continued economic embargo by the USA, which has hardened Cuba's determination to maintain its socialist values and kept Fidel Castro firmly in power for almost 50 years. The new President, Fidel's brother Raúl, is likely to maintain the status quo.

The political system

Cuba is a communist republic with a centrally planned economy. The present Constitution of the Republic of Cuba was approved by 98 per cent of legal voters. The supreme government body is the National Assembly of the People's Power, which appoints the State Council, the Council of Ministers and the president of the State Council, who is Head of State and Government (currently Raúl Castro).

There are 589 members of the National Assembly of the People's Power, who are elected by universal suffrage every five years. Below the National Assembly are the Provincial and Municipal Assemblies which are elected in the same way, every two and a half years. It is primarily through the delegates in these assemblies that the people express their wishes.

The only political party is the Cuban Communist Party, and citizens directly elect candidates. Decision-making is done by the National Assembly which passes all laws, based on the 'advice' of the President. It is called a democratic process, based on the ideal of 'the right of the people to eat, to be educated and to be treated in hospitals'. However, the National Assembly does not have the power to remove the President.

Administrative districts

The island has 14 provinces plus the special municipality of the Isla de la Juventud. For economic, political and administrative purposes, Cuba is divided into 169 municipalities. The capitals of the 14 provinces are as follows: Santiago de Cuba, Holguín, Guantánamo, Bayamo, Las Tunas, Camagüey, Ciego de Ávila, Sancti Spíritus, Santa Clara, Cienfuegos, Matanzas, Pinar del Río and Havana (the latter being two provinces).

More flexibility

In 1992 various amendments were introduced to the Cuban Constitution, among them the guaranteeing of foreign investments, more flexibility in foreign trade, and the introduction of direct election by universal suffrage of deputies to the National Assembly. This relaxation of socialist principles forms part of a more pragmatic approach by the Cuban government, which realised the urgent need for foreign investment and foreign earnings in the wake of the disintegration of the Soviet Union, its most important ally.

Political theory

The theory behind Cuba's political system is based on the ideals of the Communist Party, which works for the interests of the working class, and whose aim is to achieve a society in which everyone is equal, has the same rights, and can fulfil their dreams in a collective way. The important distinction between this and the capitalist path is that here, the collective is more important than the individual. This concept is the cause of much frustration among ambitious and liberal Cubans. The other important strand in Cuba's political ideals is the thinking of José Martí, whose ideals of freedom, happiness and independence continue to inspire Cubans today.

Achievements of the Revolution

The political system has underpinned several important achievements. Education in Cuba is free and compulsory up to the 9th grade (age 14–15). In 1961 Cuba carried out a national campaign against illiteracy, and today every adult can read and write. There are polytechnics and specialised institutes in all provinces, and also a number of universities.

Cuba's system of primary health care covers the entire country and is considered to be unique in Latin America. Health services are free for all Cubans. The infant mortality rate is 7.1 per thousand live births, and life expectancy at birth is 75.2 years, figures that are better than those of many developed countries. Cuban medicine is very advanced, powered by the many scientific research and production companies in the country. Cuba was among the first countries to produce interferon, and its vaccines against meningitis B and C, and hepatitis B, are unique in the world. The country is one of the world's leading exporters of pharmaceuticals.

The future

Fidel Castro fell ill and needed major surgery in July 2006, and his brother Raúl took over as acting President. In February 2008, Fidel did not stand again as President and Commander-in-Chief, and Raúl's election as his successor was hardly a surprise. In March 2008, Raúl introduced much-needed reforms to let farmers cultivate idle land and to allow people to buy electronic goods, rent cars and use tourist hotels and all the beaches. However, Cuba looks set to continue its communist course for the foreseeable future.

Fidel Castro – *El Jefe*

For nearly 50 years until his retirement in 2008, Fidel Castro Ruz was the dominant figure in Cuban history. In 1959 he was the youngest ruler, and he has been the longest serving head of government in the world. Despite hundreds of assassination attempts since the 1960s, he saw eight US presidents come and go, and did not succumb to serious illness until 2006. Castro has personified the Cuban state for decades: as Alejo Carpentier wrote, 'he accomplished what José Martí had promised'.

Many tourists come to Cuba to see the country 'before Castro dies'. Even with Cuba now under his brother Raúl's leadership, Castro is still expected to exert considerable influence. Cubans refer to him as 'Fidel' in reverential tones.

Born in Birán in eastern Cuba on 13 August 1926, his father was originally from Galicia in Spain, and the young Fidel studied with the Jesuits before taking a degree in law. After realising that peaceful protest would not bring about change, he took up the revolutionary cause, and was one of 150 insurgents who attempted to storm the Moncada Barracks in 1953. Many were captured and executed, but Castro and several others escaped, later to be caught and imprisoned on the Isla de la Juventud. Castro's defence speech during the trial was to become the basis of a reform programme and a summary of Castro's revolutionary thinking, named after the famous last sentence: 'History will absolve me.'

A poster congratulates Castro on his 80th birthday

After imprisonment and then exile, he launched his second armed uprising in 1956, landing in Cuba on the now legendary *Granma* cabin cruiser. Although the uprising was crushed, Castro, along with his brother Raúl and Che Guevara, escaped into the Sierra Maestra mountains where they gradually built up popular support and began guerrilla warfare against the US-backed dictatorship of Batista. By 1959, a general revolt had succeeded in overthrowing the dictatorship. After initially declining office, Castro became supreme *comandante*, president and all-round *jefe* (chief), a post that he held for almost 50 years.

His once-famous four-hour speeches and cigar smoking had to cease following the illness that struck him down in the summer of 2006. Yet he has always said that he wants his ideals to outlive him: 'Men pass away, people stay; men pass away, ideas live on.'

Castro and his revolutionaries

People and religion

The population of Cuba is over 11.3 million inhabitants, and over 76 per cent live in urban areas. Population density is 102 inhabitants per square km (264 per square mile) and the most densely populated provinces are the City of Havana with a population of 2.2 million, Santiago de Cuba with 1 million and Holguín with roughly the same.

The people of Cuba are culturally mixed, resulting from the intermingling of white Europeans (especially Spanish), blacks descended from African slaves, and Asians descended from the Chinese community. It is estimated that over half of all Cubans are people of mixed race. Cubans are generally very sociable, talkative and outgoing, with a love of laughter and having fun.

There is no real boundary between the home and the street, with many house doors remaining open and much socialising in the street or on balconies. Many people spend the whole day outside, chatting, playing dominoes, flirting or just sitting watching the world go by. The family plays a central role in the lives of most Cubans, with much socialising in the evenings, watching TV or sitting in rocking chairs and talking.

Music plays an important part in people's lives, and little excuse is needed to dance and start a party. One of the most important celebrations is the debut of 15-year-olds in society, when the girls dress up in white dresses.

Cuban society is altering rapidly because of the changing economic landscape and increasing exposure to the outside world. A new middle class is emerging, who earn CUCs in the tourist sector and who can afford many of the 'luxuries' out of reach of most Cubans. This has led to some jealousy and resentment, which is to be expected where neighbourhoods are close and everyone knows everyone else's business. While there is a relatively even distribution of wealth, with no extremes at either end, this is being put under strain by the hard currency economy, fuelled by increasing numbers of tourists who bring with them a taste of the outside world that seems so exotic and attractive to many Cubans. Castro battled the power of the American dollar. Following the establishment of tighter trade sanctions by the US, he stripped the US dollar of its legal tender status in 2004. Locals now hustle for the CUC instead.

Religion

Officially, Roman Catholicism is the most widespread religion, although Afro-Cuban religions such as *santería*, which mix black African beliefs with Catholicism, are said to have a greater hold on Cuban culture. The visit of Pope John Paul II to Cuba in 1998 led to greater tolerance in Cuban society and an increase in the number of practising Roman Catholics. Christmas Day was reinstated as a public holiday in 1997, after 40-odd years of being abolished because it interfered with the sugar harvest.

Because slavery in Cuba was only abolished in 1886, black African traditions were kept alive to a much greater extent than in other Caribbean countries. *Santería* is the most widespread of African faiths (it is also known as *Regla de Ocha*), and is based on beliefs such as the existence of spirits that inhabit all plant life. Its origins extend back to the Yoruba slaves from Nigeria who merged their African gods with Catholic saints, so as to be able to worship them without fear of persecution from the Spaniards. Most Catholic saints now have their equivalent African gods. The main *santería* god is Olofi (Oluddumare), the creator divinity, who does not have contact with the earth but who is similar to God in Christianity. The gods who mediate between him and his followers

are called *orishas*, each of whom has his or her own characteristics.

Rituals are performed in people's homes, where altars are set up and decorated with the attributes of the god to whom they are dedicated. For example, the king of *orishas*, the warlike Changó, will have red flowers, an axe, sword, and bananas at his altar.

Induction into the *santería* religion

Culture

Cultural life in Cuba is one of the most diverse and celebrated of any Latin American country. Cuba has long used its culture as an expression of its national identity. A huge amount of talent exists in the country, developed from its Afro-Caribbean origins and Spanish colonial past, and proudly nurtured since the Revolution.

Both popular and 'high' art play an important part in Cuban culture. The government has long recognised the value of nurturing home-grown talent and developing a diverse and vibrant cultural scene. There is a strong Cuban identity in all art forms, especially music, in which Cuba has a very rich heritage (*see pp26–7*). Perhaps one of the country's biggest achievements is the promotion of the popular arts in daily life.

Ballet

Cuban ballet is highly developed, having its origins in the 1930s. The Ballet Nacional de Cuba performs at the Teatro García Lorca, as well as on the international stage. There is a biennial Festival Internacional de Ballet, held in Havana, usually in October (in even years).

The main driving force behind Cuban ballet was Alicia Alonso, a ballet dancer and director who established her own ballet company in 1955. Born in 1921, she was famous for her flawless technique and natural expressiveness, performing her most famous roles in the 1940s.

Cinema

Cuban cinema was born in 1959 upon the foundation of the Instituto Cubano

THE BUENA VISTA SOCIAL CLUB

The film and the music album called *The Buena Vista Social Club* have been credited with the explosion in popularity of Cuban music (and some say of the Cuban tourist industry, too) from 1998 when the musical documentary was released. The film is a nostalgic look at the lives of the band, whose original members are now dead or in their eighties and nineties, and their rehearsals for two international concerts. While much credit must go to the film director Wim Wenders, and to Ry Cooder for bringing the music to an international audience, the stars are the legendary musicians themselves. Ironically, the album is not for sale in Cuba, due to the nature of the recording contract and label.

del Arte y la Industria Cinematográficos (ICAIC). The ICAIC has been the driving force behind the great success of Cuban cinema since the Revolution. The golden age of Cuban cinema was the 1960s, when the revolutionary government disseminated film culture throughout the country, training film makers and technicians, and showing Cuban films to as wide an audience as possible. Cuban film directors include Santiago Alvarez, who has made many excellent documentaries, Humberto Solás (who made the classic *Lucía*) and Tomás Gutiérrez Alea, who found fame abroad with his famous 1993 film *Fresa y Chocolate* (*Strawberry and Chocolate*), which dealt with issues of dissent and homosexuality. The scarcity of resources available to Cuban film makers has been credited with the high degree of innovation, enthusiasm and non-conformism in Cuban cinema. There are many striking, modern Cuban films, dominated by satire, music and laughter, some of which are shown on long-distance bus journeys. There is an annual ICAIC film festival in Havana, which is now seen as the capital of new Latin American cinema.

Going to the cinema in Cuba is a highly recommended experience as well as being incredibly cheap. The Yara cinema in Vedado, Havana is legendary. 'Must-see' Cuban films include: *Muerte de un Burócrata* (*Death of a Bureaucrat*, Guitiérrez Alea, 1966), a comedy about petty officialdom; *Adorables Mentiras* (*Adorable Lies*, Gerardo Chijona, 1991) a poignant farce about a scriptwriter; *¡Plaff!* (*Splat!*, Juan Cantos Tabio, 1988), a social satire covering many contemporary issues; and of course the Oscar-nominated classic *Fresa y*

Teatro Roldán, Havana

Chocolate (*Strawberry and Chocolate*, Tomás Gutiérrez Alea, 1993).

Literature

The earliest known work of Cuban literature is *Espejos de Paciencia*, written by Silvestre de Balboa in 1605 about the struggles between a Spanish bishop and a French pirate.

It was not until the 19th century that Cuban literature emerged properly with its own identity. José María Heredia (1803–39) was the first of many Cuban writers involved in the struggle for independence from the Spanish, and he is credited with creating Romanticism in the Spanish language. Gertrudis Gómez de Avellaneda (1814–73) wrote the first anti-slavery novel in Latin America: entitled *Sab*, it predated *Uncle Tom's Cabin* by ten years.

The towering figure of 19th-century Cuban literature was José Martí (1853–95), an intellectual, journalist, author and poet. His best known works are *Ismaelillos* and *Versos Sencillos*, which express his nationalist ideas in elegant literary form. Many of his prophesies about Cuba's political future have been fulfilled.

The two main Cuban writers in the 20th century were Alejo Carpentier and Nicolás Guillén. Carpentier (1904–80) was one of Cuba's most original authors, and one of the first exponents of Magic Realism, through which he encouraged writers to explore their cultural roots by means of story-telling. His main works include *Los*

JOSÉ MARTÍ

One of the major icons of anti-colonialism, independence and freedom, José Martí was a poet as well as a freedom fighter. He is best known outside Cuba for the song 'Guantanamera', which utilises Martí's verse. However, his most admired work is *Versos Sencillos* (1891), which developed his style and focused on nature, self-betterment and justice. Born into a poor family in Havana, his fight against colonial injustice was partly as a result of his own suffering; while still a boy, he was sentenced to forced labour for his involvement in an 1868 conspiracy against the Spanish. After a long period of exile, he returned to Cuba in 1895 at the age of 42. He was welcomed as a political leader of the liberation movement but was tragically killed later that year, fighting in the War of Independence.

Pasos Perdidos (*The Lost Steps*), written in 1953, and *The Age of Enlightenment.* Carpentier holds a prominent position among authors in Latin America. Nicolás Guillén (1902–89) was a mulatto (of mixed race) poet who exposed the brutal conditions faced by the black population in the sugar plantations. His work *Motivos de Son* (1930) incorporates African rhythms and traditional musical genres such as *son* into his bold, experimental poetry. He was declared National Poet by Fidel Castro, and was president of the Union of Cuban Writers.

Other 20th-century literary figures include Virgilio Piñera, a reformer, and José Lezama Lima, a poet and one of the driving forces behind the *criollismo* movement in the 1940s and 1950s, who is best known for *Paradiso* (1966).

Among anti-Castro authors in exile, the leading one is Guillermo Cabrera Infante, who wrote *Tres Tristes Tigres*, a witty novel about Havana nightlife during Batista's dictatorship. After the Cuban Revolution, political restrictions were placed on writers, leading to an outcry among intellectuals in Europe. One of the leaders of the more experimental style of literature was Severo Sarduy, whose book *De dónde son los Cantantes* (*From Cuba with a Song*), written in 1967, is regarded as a classic. In recent years, writers have found it easier to express their ideas in public.

Painting

The first stage in the history of Cuban painting began in 1818 with the founding of the San Alejandro Academy of Fine Arts, after which Cuban art began to develop as a separate entity. The second stage in the 1830s was heavily influenced by the European avant-garde, but expressing the new Cuban identity. One of the most famous of Cuban paintings is *Gitana Tropical* (1929) by Víctor Manuel, which gave birth to modernism in Cuban art. The island's most famous painter is Wilfredo Lam (1902–82), who dominated the 1940s and developed his own style using cubism, African masks and surrealism, working for a while with Picasso in Paris.

Other greats during the 1930s and 1940s were Amelia Peláez and René Portocarrero, who were also greatly indebted to the European avant-garde.

In 1959 the National School of Art and the Institute for Advanced Art Studies were founded as part of a government programme of art education. The third stage of Cuban painting has been characterised by the promotion of avant-garde artists, with many talented painters emerging in recent years. International recognition of Cuban art is now growing, helped by art shows like the Havana Biennial. The best place to see colonial and modern art is at the Museo Nacional Palacio de Bellas Artes in Havana.

Culture

The Museo de Bellas Artes, Havana

Music and dance

Music is an essential part of Cuban culture and everyday life, and few countries have such a rich musical heritage. Everywhere you go, there is music, whether it be salsa from a hi-fi coming from someone's house, or a *son* group playing in the town's *casa de la trova* (music venue).

The origins of Cuban music lie in the mixture of European and African cultures which developed in the plantations, villages and ports of the island. African harmony and chorus styles as well as rhythms were absorbed into a vast melting-pot which also included European forms, particularly French and Spanish. The importance of Cuba as a trading centre, particularly in slaves, was behind the fusion of disparate musical elements into new, essentially Cuban genres.

The main type of music in Cuba is *son*, which began life in the countryside with the mixing of old songs from Spain and 'call-and-response' choruses from Africa. By the late 1920s, seven-piece bands (*septetos*) were playing *son* with vocal improvisations and a trumpet, and variations were formed, including Guajira *son*, Bolero *son* and *son* Changüí. The most famous example of these is the song 'Guantanamera' in the Guajira style. It is the *septeto* style of *son* that is mostly played in many *casas de la trova* and bars, where *trova tradicional*, ballad-style songs with guitars, can be heard.

The first truly Cuban vocal style was the Canción Habanera, which emerged in the 1830s and which produced a number of *canción* styles, including the romantic Bolero. The Nueva Trova style of *canción* reflected the path of the Cuban Revolution, and its principal exponents are Silvio Rodríguez and Pablo Milanés.

Rumba, another highly popular style, originated in poor neighbourhoods as a voice of rebellion against slavery and segregation, and developed in the ports of Havana and Matanzas. It came from a mixture of African rhythm known as the Yuka, which came from the sugar plantations, and the Spanish Décima. The main urban rumba dances are the stately *yambú* and the more sexual *guaguancó*, while Columbia is more of a country-style dance. Rumba can be a competitive style of music, with rhythms getting faster and faster, and karate moves and break-dancing sometimes finding their way in.

Another strand of Cuban music that emerged was *danzón*, which originated in Matanzas. This was based on European Contradanza with the addition of subtle African rhythms to form a kind of Cuban ragtime. Mambo and Cha cha cha styles emerged directly from *danzón* in the 1940s and 1950s. Different forms of *danzón* are played by contemporary Cuban stars such as Los Van Van and Orquesta Aragón.

Salsa was a development in the 1930s which added the Conjunto style, and the addition of conga drums, timbales, piano and more trumpets, to form more of a 'big band' sound. Salsa is said to combine *son*, rumba and *danzón*, elements of which have been borrowed from jazz and other Latin American genres.

Cuban jazz is one of the most exciting and continually developing music styles, with many young Cuban exiles leading the way in Europe. The King of Cuban Jazz is undoubtedly 'Chucho' Valdés, the virtuoso pianist whose career has spanned more than 30 years. Gonzalo Rubalcaba is another force in Cuban jazz.

The music of the Cuban carnival must be mentioned, making this the most vibrant and musical time of the year on the island. The thunderous music of conga drives the parade, with both Havana and Santiago having their own styles.

One of the earliest musical forms, the rhythm and songs of *Santería* are still strong in Cuba. Each deity has his or her own rhythm, beaten out by African bata drums, while songs in the old Yoruba language are still practised and performed.

A more recent development in Cuban music has come to be known as Timba, an urban fusion of different styles including *son*, jazz rock and funk, with lyrical themes about everyday street issues such as prostitution and the struggle to survive. The leading exponent of Timba is NG La Banda, a loose-knit group drawn from long-established bands. The music may sound chaotic, with constantly shifting rhythms, but it provides a challenging alternative to salsa music.

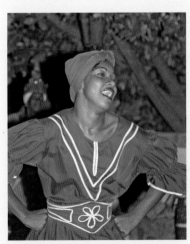

An ethnic Afro-Cuban performance in Casa de la Música, Trinidad

Festivals

There are many festivals, conferences and fiestas in Cuba throughout the year, and the Buró de Convenciones publishes a five-year list of events with full details. It can be found at Hotel Neptuno, 3rd floor, Calle 3ra corner of 70 and 74, Miramar, Havana *or at* www.cubameeting.co.cu

January
Liberation Day (national holiday)
Anniversary of the Triumph of the Revolution. *1 January.*

Feria Internacional de Artesanías, Havana
International handicrafts fair.

February
Havana
Feria Internacional del Libro
Book fair.

March
Festival de Monólogos y Unipersonales, Havana
Monologue acting competition.

Taller Internacional de Teatro de Títeres, Matanzas
Puppeteers' festival.

April
La Huella de España, Havana
Celebrating Spanish-Cuban culture.

Festival de Arte Danzario, Havana and Camagüey Dance festival.

May
International Workers' Day (national holiday) *1 May.*

Primero de Mayo, Havana
May Day rallies and parades.

Fiesta Nacional de la Danza, Santa Clara
Local dance festival.

June
Encuentro de Bandas de Concierto, Bayamo
Outdoor concerts.

Havana Carnival
Parades and music.

Jornada Cucalambeana, Encuentro Festival Iberoamericano de la Décima, Las Tunas.
Festival of Cuban rural culture.

July

Festivities in honour of the 26 July 1953 attack on Moncada Garrison (national holiday). *25, 26 and 27 July.*

Fiesta del Fuego, Santiago de Cuba
Culture of Caribbean nations.

Santiago Carnival

August

Festival Internacional de Música Popular 'Benny Moré', Cienfuegos

September

Fiesta de la Virgen de la Caridad del Cobre, Santiago de Cuba
Pilgrimage.

Festival de Teatro de La Habana

October

Beginning of the Wars of Independence (national holiday). *10 October.*

Festival de La Habana de Música Contemporánea

Fiesta de la Cultura Iberoamericana, Holguín
Spanish culture.

Festival Internacional de Ballet de La Habana

November

Salón de Arte Cubano Contemporáneo, Havana
National art fair.

Festejos de San Cristóbal de La Habana
Commemoration of the founding of the city.

Festival Internacional de Coros, Santiago de Cuba
International choir festival.

December

Christmas Day (national holiday)

Festival Internacional del Nuevo Cine Latinoamericano, Havana
Film festival.

Fiesta a la Guantanamera, Guantánamo
Afro-Cuban religion.

Parrandas de Remedios, Remedios
Folk festival.

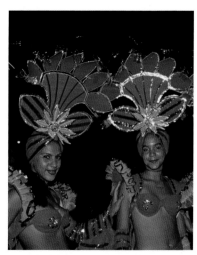

Carnival celebrations in Santiago de Cuba

Impressions

Many tourists in Cuba stay in their all-inclusive beach resorts for most of their trip, which is a shame. Those who make the effort to see the real Cuba will be rewarded with architectural gems, outstanding natural beauty, unspoilt scenery, friendly people, and the intoxicating culture of hip-swaying Cuban rhythms, delicious rum cocktails, vibrant nightlife and a passionate enjoyment of life.

Visiting Cuba is like entering a different world where even the most seasoned traveller is likely to experience some degree of culture shock. It is best to go with an open mind and a flexible attitude; otherwise you will find Cuba confusing, irrational and full of contradictions! Many of the things that we take for granted in the developed, capitalist world are not to be found in Cuba, or not given high priority. This is mainly due to the communist nature of the economic and political system, and the long period of economic isolation that the country has endured since the 1960s. However, visitors can easily overcome this initial culture shock and learn a great deal about Cuba and themselves. Cuba challenges our values, our political and economic beliefs, and enables us to appreciate the things that give us comfort in our own world, as well as appreciating the unique culture and society that Cuba has developed over the last 50 years.

The first shock that many visitors encounter happens as soon as they leave the airport upon arrival in Cuba. Many tourists take taxis or coaches from Havana airport at night, driving through the run-down, unlit areas of Havana, passing children and adults socialising or playing in the dusty streets, the doors of their houses ajar, while one glimpses a naked bulb in a living room where the noise from the television or the intoxicating rhythm of salsa music snakes its way into the street. Tourists venturing out into the streets find it hard to understand that they are quite safe, even in areas of relative urban decay.

One of the first contradictions that visitors encounter is the fact that Cuban people are generally happy, friendly and fulfilled, despite the apparent lack of material wealth and consumer goods. It is eerie at first to travel around cities where there are no advertising hoardings or posters, or shops of every description tempting us to buy. There is

Main towns and transport links

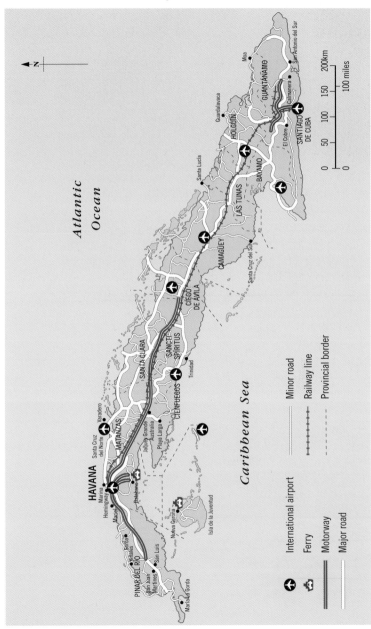

Legend:

International airport	Minor road
Ferry	Railway line
Motorway	Provincial border
Major road	

0 50 100 150 200km

0 100 miles

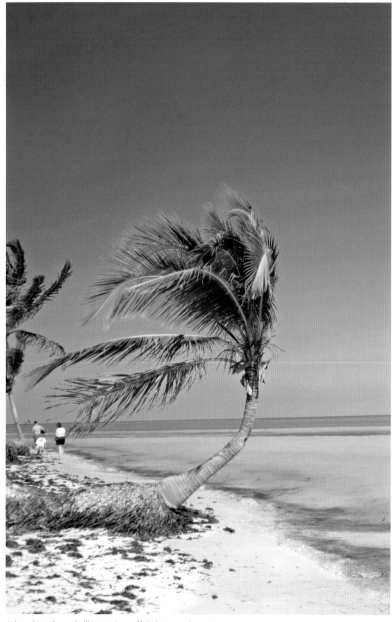

A beach at Cayo Guillermo, just off Cuba's north coast

not much of a consumer society in Cuba because the average Cuban does not have the purchasing power to buy much more than the bare essentials to keep their family fed, clothed and housed. Despite this, Cubans have a love of life and a passion for music and socialising that is contagious.

What to do and see

Cuba is a large country and many visitors underestimate its size and the amount that can be done here. Even spending a month on the island will only give you a brief taste of the riches in colonial history, scenery, wildlife and beaches that exist here. Many travellers to Cuba find that only by spending months or years living in the country do they finally start to understand the real Cuba, the one that is unseen and unknown by the tourist. However, there is much to enjoy in Cuba for those who make the effort to venture beyond the all-inclusive package holidays on the island's beach resorts.

Cuba offers a huge range of sights and activities to suit most tastes. There are the historical cities of Havana, Trinidad, Santiago de Cuba and Camagüey, there are areas of rich wildlife for nature lovers, particularly the Zapata peninsula, Guanahacabibes and Cayo Coco, and for scuba divers there is María La Gorda, Isla de la Juventud and Cayo Guillermo.

Many foreign visitors come to Cuba on a package holiday based in one of the beach resorts such as Varadero,

Guardalavaca or Cayo Coco, and venture to one of the main cities near the resort for a spot of sightseeing and culture. For those staying in Havana or Varadero on a one-week break, a visit to the province of Pinar del Río to the west of Havana, especially the Viñales Valley, is highly recommended. For a two-week break, you should definitely try to spend at least two days in Trinidad, a colonial treasure and UNESCO World Heritage Site. Also worth visiting, and within striking distance of Havana, are Las Terrazas and Soroa.

When to go

The peak tourist season in Cuba is December to mid-April, when temperatures are at their lowest (warm but not unbearable) and it is relatively dry. The storm and hurricane season begins in August and ends in November, although the number of storms does vary each year. Overall, the climate is relatively mild with lots of warm sunshine. Santiago de Cuba is always a few degrees warmer than the rest of the island, and can be unbearably hot in July and August, although this should not stop you visiting the city for the carnival.

Getting around

Havana and Santiago de Cuba are the main bases from which to see the country, with their good transport links and availability of tours to destinations near and far. Tours offer good value for money: they are a great way to visit

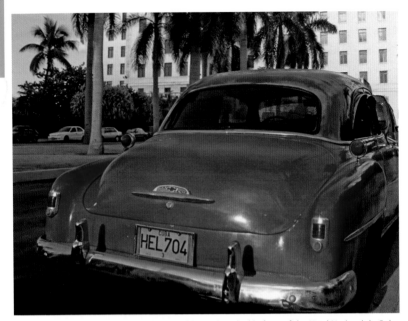

Old American cars are ubiquitous in Havana; this one is parked in front of the Hotel Nacional de Cuba

attractions out of the city centres, and many hotels have tour desks.

For the more intrepid visitor, travelling long distance by public transport is relatively efficient and cost-effective. While trains are popular, especially between Havana and Santiago de Cuba, long-haul buses are probably the most reliable and comfortable way of travelling between cities. There are internal flights around the country too, which are good value, although delays can occur. It is also possible to hire a car, which has the advantages of greater flexibility, the ability to see more of the country, less cost if there are more than two of you, and the fact that the road traffic is very

light. This must be weighed up against the disadvantages of driving in Cuba: poor road signage means that it is easy to get lost, there is a relative scarcity of petrol stations, and you run the risk of breaking down.

How to behave

Cuba has made great strides in the field of tourism over the last decade: there is now a large range of accommodation suitable for all budgets, and getting around the island is fairly easy. While there is not much in the way of tour brochures and promotional material to take away, there are many travel agencies and tour desks that are very helpful. As with everything in Cuba, it is best to be flexible, patient and good-natured about the level of service. There can be a fair amount of bureaucracy and inefficiency, and visitors can be nonplussed by the mechanisms for getting things done. For example, museums may be shut for reasons that no one can explain, transport may not be available, and things happen with a seemingly invisible hand presiding over them. A smile and a friendly approach will always help, as Cubans are generally very eager to please. As they say in Cuba, 'todo se resuelve' (everything will resolve itself). Those expecting European or North American levels of service and efficiency will have a frustrating time.

The language

Cubans are a proud people, and for the most part want to create a good impression on foreigners. They will try to speak English where they can, but a few words of Spanish, even if spoken badly, will go a long way in breaking the ice. Learning some Spanish should

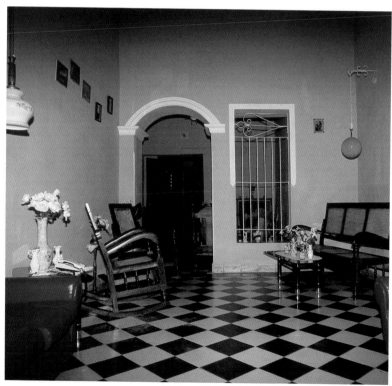

Accommodation in a *casa particular* such as this is often sought by tourists (*see p170*)

be the main priority for prospective visitors to Cuba, and the rewards make it worth the effort. Not only does it make it much easier to get around and do things, but it also enables you to get to know Cubans on a more human level and to understand the country better.

Cubans speak Spanish relatively fast in comparison with people in other Latin American countries, with some consonants dropped, especially at the end of words. Young people are more likely to speak good English, and the learning of foreign languages is being encouraged in Cuba, especially for people who are hoping to work in the tourist sector.

Jineterismo and crime

Compared to most countries in the Americas, Cuba is safe and peaceful. One can walk in the streets at night in Cuban cities, and thefts or other crimes against tourists are rare. This is because the punishments are severe for any activity that might harm tourism, and because there is not the level of extreme poverty that is found in other Latin American countries. However, the strong growth in tourism and the fluctuating state of the Cuban economy have made petty crime more common. Bear in mind that the average Cuban will earn about $10–$15 (£6–£8) per month, so any method of obtaining this kind of money in one go is naturally very tempting. It is best to take the same precautions against petty crime in

Cuba as one does at home. Never carry large amounts of money with you, leave valuables at your hotel, and keep handbags and day-rucksacks on your front rather than your back, especially in crowded areas.

One phenomenon that has become prevalent in recent years is *jineterismo*. This, in effect, is the practice of living off tourists through the creation of a friendship or relationship. It can range from a man in the street offering anything from cheap cigars, a meal or room for the night, or a *chica* (prostitute), or the *jinetero* or *jinetera* befriending you and offering to help you in any way possible. Many of these 'chance' encounters begin with a question such as 'Where you from, my friend?' One way of recognising a *jinetero* is to judge the effort and speed with which the person tries to establish a friendship, which, at its worst, can feel uncomfortable and pressurising. However, most prospective *jineteros* are harmless and will give up if you are firm but polite, and especially if you can speak some Spanish. The police are cracking down on prostitution and other associations between locals and tourists, and it is common for police officers, in uniform or plain clothes, to operate in tourist areas at night.

Lifestyle

Adapting to the Cuban way of life is one of the pleasures of visiting the country. Cubans enjoy their nightlife, whether it is at a local salsa or *son* venue, walking the streets of the city with friends, or just sitting on the patio at home, enjoying the night-time breeze and watching the activity in the street. Music forms an important part of the Cuban lifestyle, and there is a bewildering array of musical styles, from traditional salsa and *son*, to *charanga* and the more African beats of rumba.

It must be said that Cuba is not noted for its cuisine, due to the economic blockade of the island by the USA and its Latin American partners, which has robbed the island of most of its imported food. Most meals consist of rice with beans, a simple salad, cooked meat (chicken, pork or beef) and either fried plantain or potato. Food cooked in *casas particulares* is typically much better than that in restaurants, and owners will endeavour to buy different types of food in private markets.

Rum is the most popular drink on the island, whether neat, with Coke and ice, or other mixes. The *mojito* is a firm favourite and must be tried, if only once. Once you experience a good night out in Cuba with music, dance and rum, you will already feel that you know the island just that bit better.

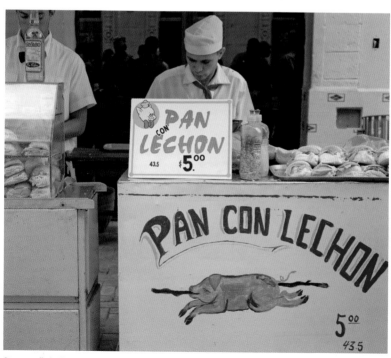

Street stalls in Havana

Havana

Havana is emerging as one of the most colourful and vibrant capital cities in the Caribbean, and is probably the finest example of a Spanish colonial city in the Americas. After decades of neglect, the old city was declared a UNESCO World Heritage Site in 1982, and is undergoing a huge facelift, mostly with foreign investment, to restore it to its former architectural glory. It now draws ever-increasing numbers of tourists, attracted by its splendid architecture, bustling nightlife and hugely nostalgic atmosphere.

Before the Revolution in 1959, Havana attracted the megastars of the day to its casinos, glamorous nightlife and hedonistic atmosphere. Since then, time has taken its toll both on the buildings and the economy. There may be no casinos now, but Havana's bars and clubs, with their thriving music scene, are still a major draw for foreigners and Cubans alike.

It must be said that Havana is not a modern city, and visitors expecting fine cuisine and high-class shopping will be disappointed. Many newly arrived visitors are taken aback by the run-down nature of most of the city and

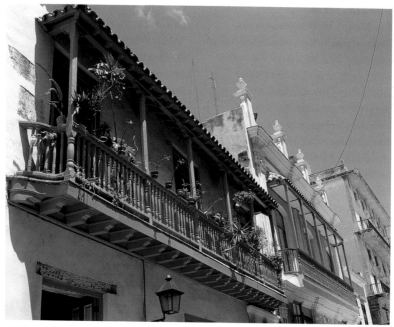

A 17th-century balcony in Calle Obispo

the poor living conditions of many Cubans. The lack of advertising hoardings or commercial districts is also unsettling at first. On the other hand, the socialist way of life means that the city is unhindered by materialistic pressures, and has a laid-back, contented pace of life.

Havana was founded in 1519, and is situated at the mouth of a deep bay. The city is split into 15 municipalities, of which three contain the main attractions: Habana Vieja (Old Havana) which is the colonial centre, Centro Havana (Central Havana) and Vedado. These three areas are linked by the Malecón, a long road along the seafront.

PIRATES AND CORSAIRS

From the second half of the 16th century to the end of the 17th, the Spanish had many enemies wishing to share in their newly found wealth in the New World. Pirates were self-employed voyagers who sailed under no nation's flag. Buccaneers such as the Welshman Henry Morgan, the British Sir Francis Drake, and the Frenchman Jacques de Sores, who sacked Havana in 1555, had the permission of their monarch to attack other countries' ships. Corsairs were mercenary ships commissioned and financed by nation states, particularly Britain, France and the Netherlands. These attacks on Spanish galleons and ports led to the building of the impressive fortifications around the main ports, including those in Havana and Santiago de Cuba.

HABANA VIEJA

The historic heart of Havana was declared part of the 'cultural heritage of humanity' by UNESCO in 1982. After many years of neglect, the former splendour of this district is being restored by the Superintendent of Cultural Heritage, with the aid of foreign investment. This area is characterised by Hispanic-Andalusian architecture, and is in fact the largest colonial centre in Latin America.

Several days can be spent in Habana Vieja, strolling around the streets or waterfront, and taking in the atmosphere in open-air cafés and restaurants (and being serenaded by visiting musicians). Don't forget to look up at the balconies, which are just as fascinating as life on the ground.

Around the Plaza de Armas

This beautiful square is the heart of the colonial centre and an excellent starting point for exploring Habana Vieja. The elegant, spacious square is lined with baroque buildings and is full of tropical vegetation. It attracts throngs of visitors and locals alike, who relax on benches or browse around the second-hand book market.

The plaza was built in the 1600s to replace the old Plaza Mayor, the core of Havana's religious, administrative and military life. In the 18th and 19th centuries it became a favourite area for rich Havana citizens to walk around or enjoy carriage rides. The statue in the centre of the square is of Carlos Manuel de Céspedes.

Around the square and in the adjoining streets are some of the most important buildings and sights in the old city, where much careful restoration work has been carried out in recent years.

Calle Obispo

This street is lined with beautiful colonial buildings dating from the 16th to the 19th centuries, including old pharmacies and historic shops. It is an ideal street to stroll down when walking eastwards from the Havana Centro district to Habana Vieja.

Castillo de la Real Fuerza

This 16th-century castle is the oldest military construction in Havana, and the second oldest fort in the New World. Built to protect the city from pirate attacks, it has a broad moat, angular ramparts and a tower with great views. Closed at the time of going to press, it is due to reopen with a museum of treasure retrieved from sunken ships sometime in 2008.
Plaza de Armas, between O'Reilly and Avenida del Puerto. Tel: 616130. Open: daily 9am–7pm. Small admission charge.

Museo de la Ciudad
(Palacio de los Capitanes Generales)

On the west side of the Plaza de Armas is the former Palacio de los Capitanes Generales, a superb example of colonial baroque architecture. The

Habana Vieja

Spanish governors and presidents lived here from its construction in 1780. It now houses the history museum of the city of Havana, comprising a collection of 19th-century furnishings and memorabilia from the Spanish colonial period. The courtyard contains a statue of Columbus and huge royal palms.

The key sights within the museum include the Cenotaph from the Parroquial Mayor Church, La Giraldilla (the oldest bronze statue in Cuba) and Salón de los Espejos (a 19th-century salon filled with Venetian mirrors).

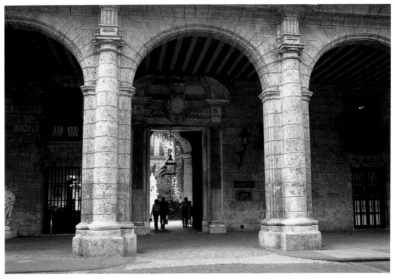

The baroque splendour of Palacio de los Capitanes Generales

Calle Tacón 1, west side of Plaza de Armas. Tel: 615779. Open: daily 9am–6pm. Admission charge, separate charges for guided visits and use of cameras/videos, under-12s free.

El Templete

This church is housed in a small neoclassical building built in 1828, and evokes memories of the city's foundation (*see p49*). A column in front of the building commemorates the spot where the first Mass was said in 1519 under a ceiba tree, an occasion that is celebrated here every 16 November. All guided tours of La Habana Vieja start here.

Northeast corner of the Plaza de Armas, between Calle Baratillo and O'Reilly. Open: daily 8.30am–6.30pm.

Plaza de la Catedral

Plaza de la Catedral is a beautiful square, with a relaxed atmosphere, where women in colonial costume stroll under the arcades and read fortunes, and with a restaurant where you can listen to live music. The impressive façade of San Cristóbal cathedral dominates the square.

In 1592 the first Spanish aqueduct in the New World was built here, providing water to local residents and ships docking in the harbour. The cathedral and aristocratic buildings were built in the 18th century.

La Bodeguita del Medio

This little bar and restaurant is the most famous in Havana, thanks to the novelist Ernest Hemingway who was a regular here. Meaning 'little shop in the middle', it is exactly halfway along the block. It was in fact founded as a food shop, but soon a bar was added and became a haunt for intellectuals and the stars of the day, including Hemingway, Nat King Cole and the writer Gabriel García Márquez. It is always busy, and is constantly besieged by tour groups. *Calle Empedrado 207, a few steps from the cathedral. Tel: 8668857. Open: daily 10.30am–midnight.*

Catedral de San Cristóbal

The Cuban author Alejo Carpentier described the beautiful baroque façade of this cathedral as 'music turned into stone'. It is certainly grandiose, with two large, asymmetrical bell towers and an abundance of niches and columns. Construction of the cathedral began in 1748 under the Jesuits, but it only received its current name in 1796 when, according to popular belief, the relics of Christopher Columbus were housed here until 1898. In comparison to the façade, the neoclassical interior is disappointing.
Calle Empedrado 156. Tel: 8617771. Open Mon–Fri 10.30am–3pm, Sat 10.30am–2pm, Sun 9am–noon, Mass Mon–Fri 8pm, Sat 5pm, Sun 10.30am. Admission charge for the cathedral tower.

Museo de Arte Colonial

This 18th-century colonial mansion houses a fascinating museum of Colonial art, and contains furniture, chandeliers, porcelain and other items from various 18th- and 19th-century

Making *mojitos* in the Bodeguita del Medio

aristocratic houses in Havana, combining European, Creole and colonial traditions. It also includes an exquisite collection of stained-glass windows (*mediopunto*).
Calle San Ignacio 61. Tel: 8626440. Open: daily 9am–6.30pm. Admission charge, plus charges for tours and taking photos.

Plaza de San Francisco

With a little imagination, from this square you can view the port in days gone by, full of galleons loaded with gold and other cargo, about to set sail for Spain. The original commercial nature of this Andalusian-style square can be seen in two buildings, the old customs house (Aduana General de la República) and the former stock exchange (Lonja del Comercio).

Basílica Menor de San Francisco de Asís

The most important feature of the square is this massive military-looking building, built in the 18th century. The bell tower (*campanario*) has marvellous views of the city and the port, and was at the time a landmark for returning voyagers and a lookout for pirates. The building is now used as a concert hall for choral and chamber music. The convent is now a museum of holy art.
Calle Oficios. Tel: 8629683. Museum open daily 9am–6.30pm. Admission charge. Tickets for concerts are available here, under-12s free.

Fuente de los Leones

Set in the middle of the square, this fountain is modelled on one found in the Alhambra, in Granada, Spain. It was donated to the city in 1836, and for many years it supplied the ships docked here with drinking water.

Other sights in Habana Vieja
Convento de Santa Clara

One of the oldest and most typical of colonial religious buildings in the New World, the convent covers four blocks of

The stunningly restored Plaza Vieja

Habana Vieja. The plain exterior belies a more extravagant interior, with carefully preserved cloisters, nuns' cells and patios overflowing with vegetation.

It was founded in 1644 by nuns from Cartagena in Colombia, and offered refuge to the poorer girls of the city. For a time, between 1919 and 1982, the building housed the Ministry of Public Works, but it was then decided to return the building to its former glory, a project which still continues today.

Calle Cuba 610, between Calles Sol and Luz. Tel: 8615043. Open: Tue–Sat 9am–4.30pm, Sun 9am–12.30pm. Admission charge.

Feria del Tacón

An interesting and colourful stroll can be had around this, the largest craft market in the city, even if you don't buy anything. The list of products available, from souvenirs to carvings and jewellery, is endless, and you may find yourself spending longer here than you anticipated! It does get very warm here, so remember to bring drinks to cool you down.

Calle Tacón, between Chacón and Empedrado, close to Plaza de la Catedral. Open: Wed–Sat 10am–6pm.

Fundación Havana Club

Visitors can see the production process in this distillery of the most famous brand of Cuban rum. The fermentation, distillation, filtering and ageing processes are all covered

THE BEST VIEWS OF HAVANA

1 Looking from the top-floor swimming pool of the Hotel Saratoga towards the Capitol building in the morning light.
2 From José Martí Memorial, Plaza de la Revolución, looking over Old Havana.
3 Sitting in the garden terrace at the Hotel Nacional, looking down on the Malecón in the softening rays of the late-afternoon sun.
4 Looking westwards towards Havana from Castillo del Morro, best seen in the morning.
5 From the Hotel Havana Libre top-floor restaurant in the afternoon or early evening, with breathtaking views over the whole city.

in the tour, with the chance to taste samples of what one Cuban writer described as 'the cheerful child of sugar cane'.

Calle San Pedro 262, between Sol and Muralla. Tel: 8618051. Open: Mon–Thur 9am–5pm, Fri & Sat 9am–4pm, Sun 10am–4pm. Admission charge includes guide and drink.

Plaza Vieja

This square is dazzling in its restored Spanish colonial beauty. It was originally laid out in 1559 and known as 'New Square', and it was the city's main public square until the 19th century. It has many fine buildings with elegant balconies overlooking the fountain in the middle. The best balcony from which to admire the view is La Casona (house of the former Conde de San Juan de Jaruco).

Walks: Habana Vieja

Habana Vieja has so many beautiful streets and buildings of interest that you can wander the streets aimlessly and bump into them at virtually every turn. However, to help recognise those of most interest and give some background detail, here are two walks that can either be taken consecutively or on separate days. They could easily fill a whole day, although a break is advised for a well-earned lunch!

WALK 1: AROUND PLAZA DE SAN FRANCISCO (*see orange route opposite*)
Allow up to 2 hours.
The tour starts in Plaza de Armas, on the south side, where Calle Oficios begins.

1 Calle Oficios
This is one of the most atmospheric streets in Havana, and recipient of much needed restoration work to its buildings. It was originally a link between the military centre of Plaza de Armas and Plaza de San Francisco, the commercial port area. There are many buildings of interest, including the **Casa de los Arabes** (ethnographic Hispanic-Arabic objects) at No 16 and the **Depósito del Automóvil** (vintage cars) at No 13.
Continuing south will bring you to Plaza de San Francisco.

2 Basilica Menor de San Francisco de Asís
The Basilica Menor de San Francisco de Asís is the most important building in this square. Built in the 18th century, it started life as home to the Franciscan community, but is now a concert hall on account of its exceptional acoustics. There are great views from the bell tower.
Back at the northwest corner of Plaza de San Francisco, take Amargura going west, and turn right onto Mercaderes.

3 Hotel Conde de Villanueva
The quiet courtyard of this charming hotel is an ideal place for a quick break from the bustle and heat of the Havana streets. It was once the residence of the Count of Villanueva in the 18th century, who promoted tobacco abroad and helped to bring the railway to Cuba. The hotel includes a cigar shop and a good restaurant.
Continue north on Mercaderes, crossing Lamparilla, and look to the left of the street.

4 Casa-Museo Simón Bolívar
Simón Bolívar is a key figure in South American history, a protestor against Spanish rule, and former resident of

Walks around Habana Vieja

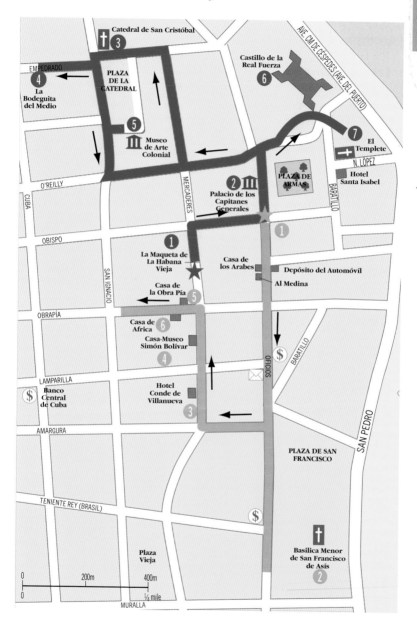

this house. There are exhibits about his life, and also some Venezuelan art.
Continue north on Mercaderes and turn left onto Obrapía.

5 Casa de la Obra Pía

The house name means 'charity', after the altruistic actions of a wealthy Spanish nobleman in the 17th century, who gave a generous dowry to five orphan girls every year, so that they could either get married or enter a convent. This yellow building is regarded as one of the finest examples of Cuban baroque architecture. The house displays furniture from the 18th and 19th centuries, and was originally built in 1665.
A few metres away on the same street, at No 157, is the Casa de África.

6 Casa de Africa

This 17th-century building exhibits many objects from the various ethnic groups that were shipped to Cuba as slaves. It includes paintings of plantation life, objects from Afro-Cuban cults, and instruments of torture. It is ironic that the building used to be the residence of a family of plantation owners on the upper floor, and a tobacco factory worked by slaves on the ground floor.

WALK 2: AROUND PLAZA DE ARMAS AND PLAZA DE LA CATEDRAL

(see green route on map, p47)
Allow 3 hours minimum.
Begin at La Maqueta de La Habana

Vieja, in Mercaderes (between Obispo and Obrapía), very near the Plaza de Armas.

1 La Maqueta de La Habana Vieja

This scale model of the city (built in the proportions of 1:500) offers an overview of the area. There are light and sound effects to replicate a day in the city.
Walk northwards on Mercaderes and turn right onto Obispo, which leads to the Plaza de Armas. On your left is the Palacio.

2 Palacio de los Capitanes Generales

Now the Museo de la Ciudad (City Museum), this fine baroque palace houses one of the key museums in Havana, offering an overview of the city's history. In front of this palace there are often displays of dance or other activities organised by the city council.
With the square in front of you, turn left to the end of the block, left again onto O'Reilly and first right onto Mercaderes. At the T-junction, turn left into Plaza de la Catedral.

3 Catedral de San Cristóbal

The baroque façade of this church, declared a national monument, is considered one of the most beautiful in Latin America. On either side are two bell towers (the west one is half as wide as the east one), which provide fine views.
Turn right out of the Cathedral and walk towards Calle Empedrado.

4 La Bodeguita del Medio

Although only small, this bar simply oozes character, and is popular with tour groups. It was a regular haunt of Ernest Hemingway, whose favourite tipple here was the *mojito* (*see p51*).

Turning back to the Plaza de la Catedral, walk to the south of the square.

5 Museo de Arte Colonial

It would be hard to find a better example of early colonial domestic architecture than this building. Dating from 1720, it houses an exhibition of colonial furniture and objects.

Turning left out of the museum, turn left onto San Ignacio and walk southwards, turning left onto O'Reilly, and walk on to the left-hand side of the Plaza de Armas. Follow the road round as it turns left.

6 Castillo de la Real Fuerza

First built in 1558, this is the oldest building in Cuba. It is worth walking around its characteristic angular ramparts, and climbing the tower to enjoy fine views of the city.

Coming out from the castle, cross the road and you will see a narrow street between the buildings. Walk down this street, Calle Enna, the narrowest and shortest street in the city, named after a general from colonial times. Keep the Plaza de Armas on your right.

7 El Templete

Another important building in Havana's history, this austere monument stands on the spot where, according to legend, the city of San Cristóbal de la Habana was founded in 1519. It was also here, under a ceiba tree (*see p42*), that the first meeting of the local government was held.

If you feel you deserve a spot of luxury, the Hotel Santa Isabel is the perfect place to enjoy good views of the Plaza de Armas with lunch or a cocktail.

Façade of the Catedral de San Cristóbal

Cuban rum

The origins of Cuban rum date back to the 1500s when alcohol was produced from sugar-cane juice. Sugar had been introduced to Cuba by Christopher Columbus, who brought sugar-cane roots from the Canary Islands.

In the 19th century, a new distillation process was introduced which considerably improved the quality of the drink, and Cuba became internationally famous for its rum. The most famous rum family was the Bacardí family, who dominated the rum industry in Cuba for nearly 100 years.

The process of rum-making begins with the dilution of molasses, the sticky amber paste which is a by-product of sugar. The diluted mixture is fermented with yeasts, then distilled and filtered to produce an *eau de vie*. After 18 months, purified water and pure alcohol are added, producing a young, clear rum known as 'Silver Dry', which is generally used in cocktails.

Other types of rum include Carta Blanca (aged for three years), Carta Oro (five years) and Añejo (seven years). Older rum is usually drunk neat or on the rocks, and is of better quality than young rum.

Cocktails became popular after 1870 when ice-making was developed in the USA, and the 'Cuba Libre' was invented when American

Bottles of seven-year-old rum and special blended rum

The display in the Fundación Havana Club in Habana Vieja

soldiers brought bottled cola drinks to Cuba at the end of the 19th century. The *daiquirí* cocktail was invented by an engineer in the Daiquirí mines in eastern Cuba, and cocktails were especially popular in the 1920s with the influx into Cuba of people from all over the world, especially Americans escaping prohibition.

Rum is an integral part of Cuban life, and it is enjoyed at parties and festivities, as well as being offered to the gods of *santería*. An ideal place to learn more about Cuban rum is at the distilleries of Havana Club, the most famous brand of Cuban rum. Tours begin in the courtyard of the Havana Club Foundation, in Habana Vieja.

The most famous cocktail in Cuba, which is particularly delicious in the warm climate, is the refreshing *mojito*. No two *mojitos* will taste the same, although the place to be seen drinking one is at La Bodeguita del Medio in Havana, made famous by Ernest Hemingway (*see pp42–3*).

To make a *mojito*, take a tall glass, mix together half a tablespoon of sugar, the juice of half a lime, and lightly crushed mint leaves. Add 43ml (1½fl oz) of light dry rum, ice cubes and top up with soda water. Garnish it with a mint leaf and serve with a straw. Other rum cocktails that tourists will come across include: the *Havana Especial* (pineapple juice, maraschino liqueur and light dry rum), *Mulata* (lime juice, crème de cacao, extra aged rum), *Ernest Hemingway Special* (lime, grapefruit juice, maraschino liqueur, light dry rum, and served like a *daiquirí*).

CENTRO HABANA

The boundary between Old Havana and central Havana (Centro) is blurred, with Parque Central and the Capitolio lying on this border. There is certainly a change of atmosphere from Habana Vieja, and the area is less quaint, more spacious and less obviously aimed at tourists.

Parque Central

Parque Central is a popular meeting place for locals to discuss sport (mainly baseball), music and politics. Here the locals may try to befriend you by suggesting a *mojito* at a nearby bar, for which they would receive a commission from the bar.

Capitolio

One of the most imposing buildings in Latin America, the Capitolio is worth a visit in order to wander around the grandiose interior. It was built in 1929 under the regime of dictator Machado in the style of the US Capitol building in Washington DC and was the seat of parliament until 1959.
Paseo de Martí (Prado) (entrance from the steps on the east side). Tel: 8615519. Open: daily 9am–7pm, although it often shuts early. Admission charge.

Gran Teatro de La Habana

With a magnificent façade, this is one of the world's largest opera houses. It was designed by Belgian architect Paul Belau and opened in 1915.
Paseo de Martí (Prado). Tel: 8613077. Open: Box office Tue–Sun 9.30am–5pm.

The Capitolio

Hotel Inglaterra

This hotel is a national monument. Although it is 19th-century neoclassical in style, it has Moorish elements, with beautiful Seville tiles inside.
Paseo de Martí (Prado) 416, on the corner of San Rafael. Tel: 8608595.

Paseo de Martí (Prado)

This picturesque boulevard, laid out in 1772 outside the city walls, is ideal for a gentle stroll in the shade of the trees.
Paseo de Martí (Prado) runs north from Parque Central to the Castilla de la Punta by the sea.

Other sights in Centro Habana
Museo Nacional de Bellas Artes

This is perhaps the finest museum in Cuba with almost 50,000 works of art from all over the world. Its collections are divided between the original *palacio* and the Palacio del Centro Asturiano, three blocks away by the Parque Central. Highlights include works by Gainsborough, Velázquez and Murillo.

Palacio (original building) on Trocadero, between Zulueta and Avenida de las Misiones. Features Cuban art. Tel: 8613858. Open: Tue–Sat 10am–6pm, Sun 10am–2pm. Admission charge, under-12s free. Centro Asturiano on San Rafael, between Zulueta and Avenida de las Misiones. Features world art. Admission details as above.

Museo de la Revolución

It is surely no coincidence that the museum recounting the history of the Cuban Revolution is in the former presidential palace of the US-backed dictator Batista. The museum shows Cuba's political development, from the slave uprisings to the period of cooperation with the former Soviet Union. The grounds house the yacht *Granma*, which carried Castro and his companions to launch the revolution in 1956, and the tank used to attack US ships in the Bay of Pigs in 1961.

Calle Refugio, between Avenida de las Misiones and Zulueta. Tel: 8624092. Open: daily 10am–5pm. Admission charge, plus charge for a recommended guided tour (as displays are mostly in Spanish), under-12s free.

Walk: Centro Habana

While the romantic little streets of Habana Vieja mostly hark back nostalgically to the colonial days of the 19th century, Centro relates mostly to the first half of the 20th century. It has a different atmosphere which is more gritty and in a sense more reflective of life in Cuba's capital city.

Allow 3 hours for the walk, although it can be extended to include a walk down the Malecón, the city's seafront.

1 Capitolio

The Capitol building is a symbol of the city, dominating the area with its neoclassical elegance. The home of the government from its opening in 1932 until 1959, the sumptuous interior is well worth visiting, and is an ideal spot for a drink in the café.
At the bottom of the steps, turn left and walk up Paseo de Martí (Prado) towards the grand building in front of you.

2 Gran Teatro de La Habana

The impressive façade of this concert hall and theatre includes four sculpture groups depicting Charity, Education, Music and Theatre.
Continue walking north, past Calle San Rafael on your left.

3 Hotel Inglaterra

Despite the British name, this 19th-century hotel is definitely inspired by Spain. Soak up the atmosphere in one of its four cafés and restaurants.
From the hotel, cross to the park opposite.

4 Parque Central

This pleasant park is surrounded by grand hotels and historic buildings, and is a gathering place for locals to relax under the shady trees. The statue in the centre is of José Martí.
Facing north, you can see the long boulevard of Paseo de Martí.

5 Paseo de Martí (Prado)

Ideal for a stroll at any time of day, this lovely boulevard continues all the way up to the seafront. There are many attractive buildings.
Continue walking north, and look right after passing Calle Empedrado.

6 Hotel Sevilla

This Moorish building is a historic hotel which first opened in 1908. The bar and restaurant on the top floor is a great spot from which to enjoy the views over the Malecón.
Continue to the end of the Prado towards the Castillo de la Punta, where the Malecón begins, and turn left.

7 Malecón

This seafront promenade represents Havana more than any other place. It is also a gathering point for locals. Some of the buildings along it are being restored, while others are losing the battle against the destructive sea air. The Malecón continues for 7km (just over 4 miles) from the colonial centre through Centro and into Vedado.

Architecture

In the 16th century a network of fortresses was established around the coast of Cuba to protect Spanish possessions from pirate attacks. Tourists can visit many of these fortresses, including the Castillo de la Real Fuerza in Havana.

The oldest house in Cuba, Diego de Velázquez's residence in Santiago de Cuba, was built in 1522. Simple wooden dwellings built before this time were gradually replaced by stone-built *mudéjar*-style houses. By the 17th century, many private homes had thick walls, tiled roofs and shuttered windows, all of which gave protection from the tropical sun and heavy rain. Central courtyards and wooden balconies reflected Spanish influence.

The 18th century is seen as the golden age of Cuban architecture, characterised by the baroque style imported from Europe. The most notable baroque building in Havana is the Cathedral, built in 1777, and many churches were built during the 17th and 18th centuries, reflecting the great power of the church at that time. Highlights of civic baroque architecture in Havana include the Palacio de los Capitanes Generales and the Palacio del Segundo Cabo. The *mediopunto* style of stained-glass

The baroque Cathedral, Havana

windows was developed in the mid 18th century to protect houses from the tropical sun.

Neoclassical architecture was predominant in the 19th century, characterised by porticoes with columns and lintels, wrought iron and decoration inspired by classical antiquity and the Renaissance. The first neoclassical building in Havana was the Templete, a small doric temple in the Plaza de Armas. Other good examples of this style are the Palacio de Aldama in Havana and the Teatro Santo in Matanzas.

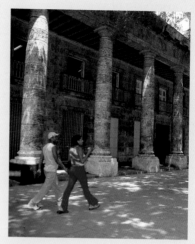

The 19th-century neoclassical Palacio de Aldama, Havana

Between the 19th and 20th centuries, there was a mix of architectural styles, in both public and private buildings. The most notable of these are the Capitolio in Havana, the neo-Moorish Palacio de Valle in Cienfuegos and the splendid Havana mansions at Paseo and Calle 17, including the Casa de la Amistad.

Art nouveau and art deco architecture were popular in the early 20th century. The best example is the sumptuous Edificio Bacardí in Habana Vieja, while other examples can be seen on the Malecón in Havana.

The most popular architect in the 1950s was Aquiles Capablanca, who was inspired by Le Corbusier, and his Tribunal de Cuentas in Havana is one of the most admired 20th-century buildings in Latin America. Another stunning building is the Tropicana nightclub in Miramar, built in 1952 by Max Borges Jr. Tall skyscrapers were also built around this time, including the Habana Libre and Riviera hotels.

The Revolution saw the conversion of old private buildings for public use rather than the construction of new buildings, for example, the Moncada Garrison in Santiago which is now a school and museum. The influence of Soviet architecture can also be seen, with adaptations to the buildings to take account of the Cuban climate. Many state-run hotels were built in the 1960s and 1970s.

A good overview of the development of Havana's architecture can be obtained by viewing the scale model of the city which is situated at *La Maqueta de La Habana, Calle 28 No 113, between Calles 1 and 3*.

VEDADO AND PLAZA

The areas of Vedado and Plaza (the area around Plaza de la Revolución) fulfil many roles. Firstly, they represent the city's political and cultural centre, containing Plaza de la Revolución, the venue for major celebrations and political gatherings. They also contain many buildings of interest, from early 20th-century mansions to large hotels made famous in the 1950s through their glamour and their links with the mafia. Vedado is the place to be for the best nightlife and cultural events.

The name Vedado means 'forbidden' in Spanish, a reference to its 16th-century origins, when it was forbidden to build houses in the area, so that a full view of approaching pirates or invaders could be had. Vedado expanded extensively from the late 19th century, when many of the city's leading families set up residence in the area.

Vedado sights
Memorial José Martí
While the monument itself is not to everyone's taste, the views from the top – the monument is over 100m (328ft) tall – and the impressive museum at the base make this an unmissable sight in modern Havana. Work on the monument began in 1953, on the 100th anniversary of the birth of Cuba's national hero. The memorial at the base contains memorabilia and portraits of Martí, while the lobby features some of the patriot's thoughts.

The José Martí memorial

Plaza de la Revolución. Tel: 592351. Open: Mon–Sat 9am–5pm. Admission charge, under-12s free.

Museo Nacional de Artes Decorativas
This impressive museum is worth visiting for its French rococo and Louis XV furnishings, its lovely inner gardens, and the Regency-inspired dining room, complete with a grand dinner service owned by dictator Batista. This was the former residence of the Countess de Revilla de Camargo, one of the wealthiest Cuban women of the 20th century, who enjoyed collecting fine art and holding elegant society dinners. It houses some beautiful art, furniture and porcelain from Europe and the Far East, including a desk that once belonged to

Marie Antoinette. The pink marble art deco bathroom is remarkable.

No 502, Calle 17, corner of Calle E.
Tel: 8308037. Open: Tue–Sat 11am–6.30pm. Admission charge, under-12s free.

Necrópolis Cristóbal Colón

One of the largest cemeteries in the world, the Necrópolis Colón houses a wealth of funerary art and is a national monument. Also known as Cementerio Colón (Columbus Cemetery), it contains 2 million graves, equal to the city's current population. Dating from 1886, it was designed by Spanish architect Calixto de Loira and the main entrance features a statue in Carrara marble of the three virtues, Faith, Hope and Charity, sculpted in 1904.

Entrance is on Zapata and Calle 12.

Tel: 8304517. Open: daily 9am–5pm.
Admission charge, includes tour.

Plaza de la Revolución

This massive square is not one of the most beautiful, but is worth visiting for its importance, both historically and politically. It was originally designed in 1952 and most of the buildings around it are from this time. It is here that the major rallies and speeches in Havana are held, and the square can hold around 1 million people. The first rally was held in January 1959 following victory in the Cuban Revolution and Pope John Paul II celebrated Mass here in January 1998.

Every year on the morning of 1 May, Fidel Castro used to address a million people to celebrate International Labour Day.

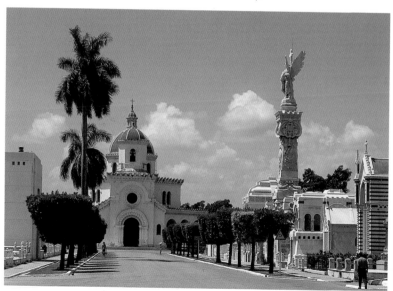

The national monument of Necrópolis Cristóbal Colón

Walk: Vedado district, Havana

Vedado is a busy, largely residential area of broad avenues, with a real mix of architectural styles, from ugly 1950s high-rises to crumbling neoclassical mansions. The area houses many government offices as well as the university, which makes it a lively part of town, especially at night. The main avenue here is Calle 23, better known as La Rampa, modern Havana's best-known street.

Allow 2½ hours.

The walk starts at Hotel Nacional. This walk does not include any museums, but nevertheless provides an insight into the many different sides of modern Havana. The walk is ideal in the afternoon, when the views of Habana Vieja are at their best.

1 Hotel Nacional

Perhaps the most elegant and famous of Havana's hotels, this building has retained much of its 1930s atmosphere, when the great and the good stayed here. The bar on the ground floor has photographs of its famous guests, including some Mafia legends who financed the building of the hotel in 1930. The terrace at the end of the superb gardens has a beautiful view of virtually the whole length of the Malecón.

Walk along Calle 23 (known as La Rampa) westwards until you reach Calle N.

2 Hotel Habana Libre

The Habana Libre is one of the biggest and most visible of the city's hotels. It was inaugurated in 1958 as the most modern and decadent hotel in the capital, but was taken over by Fidel Castro when the Revolution came to Havana in January 1959, and used for a short while as his headquarters. There are some fascinating historical photos in the lobby.

Continue walking up La Rampa until you reach a park on your right with queues of people at all times of the day.

3 Coppelia ice cream

Queuing at this famous ice cream parlour is a long-established social ritual for local residents. This large glass and metal building was the famous location in one of Cuba's most well-known films *Fresa y Chocolate* (*Strawberry and Chocolate*).

Continue walking westwards on La Rampa for a couple of blocks, and look out for a park on your left.

4 Parque del Quijote

The main feature in this tree-filled area is the statue of Don Quixote. This nude figure on horseback was designed by Sergio Martínez.

Carry on walking along La Rampa and turn right when you reach Calle G (Avenida de los Presidentes). This wide avenue takes you down to the Malecón where you turn left, walking four blocks.

5 Islamada

The Feria de Malecón no longer exists but in its place is a small market, Islamada, set up by the Fondo de Bienes Culturales. It sells shoes, clothes, leather goods, paintings and other souvenirs. Some of the products are for sale in *moneda nacional*. It is open from Tuesday to Sunday, 9am–6pm.

Continue walking along the Malecón for two blocks until you reach Calle Paseo on your left. Walk up this elegant avenue until you reach Calle 15. Turn right and walk three blocks.

6 Parque John Lennon

The main feature in this peaceful park is a bronze statue of John Lennon, sitting on a bench, with words from 'Imagine' etched on the ground. Sculpted by José Villa, it was inaugurated in December 2000 by Fidel Castro. The park is sometimes used as a venue for classical guitar concerts.

Walk back towards Calle Paseo on Calle 17 (going eastwards). Once on Calle Paseo, look right.

7 Casa de la Amistad

Ideal for a drink, dinner and dancing, this cultural centre is housed in a sumptuous art deco building. Originally owned by Pedro Baró, it was given to his mistress Catalina Lasa in the early 1900s.

HAVANA ENVIRONS

There are many interesting places to visit just a taxi ride from the city centre, or as part of an organised tour booked through hotel tourist desks. These give a different picture to the one experienced in Havana alone, and are a good way of taking a break from the city.

Castillo de los Tres Reyes del Morro

This is one of the most visible landmarks in Havana, especially from the Malecón, with one of the best views back towards the city. It stands on the headland to the northeast of the city in the district of Casablanca. It was constructed in the 17th century and was one of the main fortifications built by the Spanish to protect the natural harbour from pirates and foreign invaders. It is now a museum exhibiting Cuban history since the arrival of Columbus.

Within the grounds is the **Batería de los Doce Apóstoles** (Battery of the 12 Apostles). There is a display of Afro-Cuban dancing and music every Saturday between 10 and 11pm. *You can take a taxi from the city, or take any bus going through the tunnel from San Lazaro and Avenido del Puerto. Get off at the stop after the tunnel, cross the road and climb to the left, following the path. Open: daily 10am–7pm (Museum 10am–6pm). Separate admission charges for the park, castle, lighthouse, and for photos/video.*

La Terraza was one of Hemingway's haunts in Cojímar

Cojímar

The main reason for visiting this former seaside village is to retrace the footsteps of Ernest Hemingway, who used it as the setting for his great novel *The Old Man and the Sea*, and who was a regular in the streets and bars. The village has lost some of its charm, although there are some points of interest. There is a bust of Hemingway in a small square that bears his name, a faithful copy of the one in El Floridita bar in Havana. The bust was paid for with donations from his fishermen friends. Hemingway's favourite restaurant, La Terraza, can still be visited. It is still worth a drink here, if only for a look at the photographs that cover the wall, and to sample the elegant atmosphere.

On the seafront, there is a small 17th-century fort, designed by

Giovanni Battista Antonelli, the architect of the Castillo del Morro. *Cojímar is a 15-minute taxi ride from Havana.*

Fortaleza de San Carlos de la Cabaña

A short walk from Castillo del Morro, this fortress is worth a visit if only to experience the cannon-firing ceremony (nightly at 9pm), recalling the closure of the city walls to protect it from attack. With a vertical wall of 700m (2,300ft), this famous fortress dominates the entrance to the city harbour. It was built in 1774 and was at the time the largest the Spanish had built in the Americas. In its heyday,

120 cannon were positioned within the fortress walls.

There are two museums, the first about the fortress, and the second about Che Guevara, who triumphantly took possession of the fortress in 1959 at the end of the Cuban Revolution. *The fortress is within walking distance of the Castillo del Morro or via the district of Casablanca. Open: daily 10am–10pm. Admission charge, plus charge for taking photos.*

Miramar

Located 16km (10 miles) west of the old city, Miramar is the most elegant part of Havana, as it was before the Revolution, when the city's richest

Castillo de los Tres Reyes del Morro viewed from the Malecón

inhabitants lived here. The southern part is also home to the internationally famous 'Tropicana' cabaret show, as well as excellent restaurants and music venues.

Most of the embassies and consulates are here, with lots of offices, especially for multinational joint ventures, while modern developments are springing up, catering mostly for business people. It is understandably the most desirable residential area in the city. Life in this quarter revolves around the busy Avenida 5, a broad, tree-lined avenue flanked by splendid early 20th-century villas and newer hotels.
Miramar is easily accessed by private car, taxi or bus.

Playas del Este

This is the name for the string of beaches outside Havana – one of the few cities in the world to have sizeable beaches only a 20-minute drive from the city centre. They consist of 50km (31 miles) of fine sand and clear water, offering good tourist facilities. They are a good compromise for people who want to spend some of their time at the seaside during their visit to Havana, but who don't want to travel too far. The best – and most popular – beach is Santa María del Mar, which is lined with pine and coconut trees and has very good facilities for water sports, plus a good selection of hotels.

Guanabo is a more traditional beach with small houses, restaurants and shops. At weekends, this is the liveliest place along the coast, when *Habaneros* (residents of Havana) congregate here. *The Playas del Este can be accessed by taking a taxi or hiring a private car for the day if there are two or more people;*

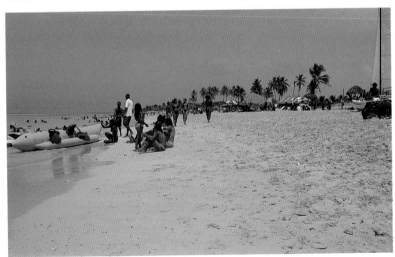

Santa María del Mar, Playas del Este

Hemingway's library at Finca Vigía

otherwise, tours can be booked at relatively low cost through tourist offices.

San Francisco de Paula (Finca Vigía)

Hemingway fans should visit the writer's only residence outside the USA, situated on the outskirts of Havana. The villa has been surprisingly well preserved, and contains virtually all the original objects and decorations. The villa was turned into a public museum in 1962, following the news of Hemingway's suicide in the USA in 1961.

There is a library with 8,000 books, hunting trophies, artworks, and even the author's pipe and typewriter. The fact that these objects have been left as they were creates a lived-in, homely atmosphere. Two curious features of the house include a cat cemetery in the garden (the author had 60 cats during his lifetime) and Hemingway's fishing boat, the *Pilar*, scene of many a drunken fishing trip.

Finca Vigía is 11km (6¹/₂ miles) from the centre of Havana. It can be visited by taxi. Tel: 910809. Open: daily except Tue 9am–4.30pm, Sun 9am–noon. Admission charge to view the interiors through open windows and doors. (There are no toilets.)

Walk: Miramar quarter, Havana

Miramar is an ideal place for a relaxing stroll where you can take in the broad avenues and elegant buildings of this relatively wealthy suburb. It also gives a contrasting impression to the more compact, run-down streets of central Havana.

Allow 3 hours.

Begin from the fort, Fuerte de Santa Dorotea de la Luna de la Chorrera, a national monument in the Vedado district, on the east side of the River Almendares. You may wish to take a break halfway through the walk for lunch or a snack – there are several good places to eat.

1 Fuerte de Santa Dorotea de la Luna de la Chorrera

This fort was crucial to the city's defence system for more than two centuries, and was built in 1645 by Giovanni Battista Antonelli, the famous Spanish military engineer.
Next to the fort is the next landmark.

2 The 1830 restaurant

The building for this restaurant was once the home of Carlos Miguel de Céspedes, the Minister of Public Works under President Machado, one of the US-backed dictators before the Revolution. The restaurant is recommended.

Walk down to Calle 11 and over the iron bridge to reach the Miramar area. Turn right and go up to Avenida 5 (Quinta Avenida).

3 Avenida 5

This broad, tranquil boulevard with shrubs and benches is flanked on both sides by large, imposing mansions built in the early 20th century. During the Revolution, these private houses were abandoned by the escaping upper classes or seized by the government who turned them into public buildings.
Walk up the Avenida, to the corner of Calle 26.

4 Iglesia de Santa Rita

There are three distinctive tall arches in the façade of this modern church, while to the left of the entrance is a statue of St Rita by Cuban sculptress Rita Longa.
Walk up to Calle 28 and turn right, then turn left on Avenida 3 (Tercera). On the right is an interesting museum.

5 Maqueta de La Habana

A great way to get an overview of the city, this scale model of Havana was opened in 1995 and is now a great attraction. The development of Havana from colonial times onwards is shown here, with different colours representing construction periods.
Continue to walk westwards along Avenida 3, then turn right to walk one block up to Avenida 1 (which runs parallel), which is the seafront. Walk left along Avenida 1 until you reach the corner of Calle 60, on your left.

6 Acuario Nacional

The city aquarium is housed in an unmistakeable pale blue building. An assortment of Caribbean and ocean habitats is reproduced, with about 3,500 specimens of sea fauna.

The most spectacular is the one with bottle-nosed dolphins, which are common in Cuban seas. Dolphin shows are performed at regular intervals. *The complex is open Tue–Sun 10am–6pm. Admission charge. You can either finish the tour here or walk eastwards along the seafront to find a peaceful spot for sunbathing.*

7 Playita 16

The water here is clear, although swimming is not recommended due to the rocky shore. This is a good place to relax and enjoy the seaside location.

Hemingway in Cuba

At various points during a typical stay in Havana, visitors will come across references to Ernest Hemingway, and there is in fact a tour that takes in the major sites of interest relating to this great American novelist. Ernest Hemingway's love affair with Cuba continued until his death in 1961. He was initially attracted by the marlin fishing, but soon gambling, prostitutes and cocktails were added to the list. He stayed in Hotel Ambos Mundos and was a regular at two bars nearby, La Bodeguita del Medio and El Floridita. In 1940 he bought a 6-hectare (15-acre) farm outside Havana, called 'Finca Vigía', in which

Hemingway with Castro at a fishing competition

he wrote some of his greatest novels. His staff included three gardeners, a cook and a man who tended the fighting cocks which Hemingway bred.

During World War II, he set up his own counter-intelligence unit with the aim of rooting out Nazi spies in Havana. He also armed his fishing boat, the *Pilar*, with bazookas and grenades, and his crew was made up of Cuban friends and Spanish exiles, as well as a radio operator supplied by the US Embassy. The boat cruised the waters around Havana searching for German U-boats. When it was apparent that these were unlikely to be found, the trips turned into a haze of drinking and fishing.

After the war, Hemingway wrote *The Old Man and the Sea*, which won him the Pulitzer Prize in 1953. In 1954 he won the Nobel Prize, and placed it at the foot of the Madonna del Cobre, near Santiago de Cuba, with the words: 'This prize belongs to Cuba, since my works were created and conceived in Cuba, with the inhabitants of Cojímar, of which I am a citizen.' Cojímar was the fishing village and setting for the novel, where he whiled away the evenings trading stories, playing dominoes and drinking rum.

It was around this time that his drinking reached its peak. It is said that he would have whisky and

Hemingway's boat *Pilar*

cocktails during the day, followed by two bottles of wine at dinner, then absinthe and whisky with soda at various casinos until the early hours. It is believed that he helped to invent the *daquirí* cocktail.

When the political situation worsened around 1958 under Batista, Hemingway returned to his home in Idaho in the USA, from where he heard the news of Castro's victory. He returned to Cuba and made a public show of his support for the Revolution, and he later met Castro during a marlin fishing tournament. In 1960 he left for Florida, committing suicide in 1961.

HAVANA EXCURSIONS

Day tours from Havana are plentiful and can be booked at the lobbies of most hotels. These are an ideal way of travelling outside Havana and seeing interesting sites without the worry of organising your own transport and guides. The tour bus will usually pick you up from your hotel and drop you back again afterwards. If you are staying in a *casa particular*, you can arrange pick-up from a nearby hotel.

Tours

While we have included a few of the more popular day trips from Havana, there are other tours which venture farther afield, for example to Viñales,

The *escaleras* (stairs) at Jaruco

Pinar del Río, Trinidad and Cienfuegos. These are generally best undertaken with an overnight stay, rather than trying to rush a visit within one day.

Jibacoa and Jaruco

Not usually included in tour brochures, Jibacoa is a pretty area within striking distance of Havana, being only 60km (37 miles) east of the city. It is well suited for snorkelling, as the reefs are close to the beach, and it is also a pleasant area for walking, as the hills extend down to the sea.

On the way back from Jibacoa, Jaruco makes an interesting diversion. From Santa Cruz del Norte, you can drive inland via the Central Camilo Cienfuegos to Jaruco, and 6km (3¹⁄₂ miles) to the west is the **Parque Escaleras de Jaruco**. These *escaleras*, or stairs, are geological formations in the limestone, set in the midst of a picturesque landscape.

Soroa

Soroa is a popular excursion that takes you to an area of natural beauty, containing a spa and resort in luxuriant hills. The biggest draw is the **Orquideario** (Orchid Garden), which is home to one of the largest orchid collections in the world. Containing more than 700 species of orchid, 250 of which are endemic, the garden was founded in 1943 by a lawyer from the Canary Islands, Tomás Felipe Camacho, and it has been declared a national monument.

The waterfall at Soroa

The route from Havana to Soroa crosses a peaceful area of cultivated fields and rural villages, while Soroa itself lies 250m (820ft) above sea level in the middle of tropical forest. The area was named after two Basque brothers who owned most of the coffee plantations in the area, and the small town of Soroa contains a holiday village with good tourist facilities. One of the main attractions is the Saltón, a spectacular waterfall on the Manantiales River.

Also of interest are the **Mirador de Venus** (Venus' viewpoint) and **Baños Romanos** (Roman Baths). You can park by the baths and walk up to the *mirador* (viewing spot), which gives fine views over the southern plains and forest-covered Sierra.

Sierra del Rosario, 81km (50 miles) southwest of the capital. Orchid Garden: Tel: 85-572558. Open: daily 9am–4pm. Admission charge. Waterfall: 10-minute walk from the Villa Soroa. Mirador: 25-minute walk from the baths. Free if walking, a charge if going by horse.

Las Terrazas

A trip to the Biosphere Reserve at Las Terrazas in the Sierra del Rosario (*see map, p74*) is a very pleasant break from the bustle of Havana city, and illustrates the efforts the government has made to develop sustainable ecology which also attracts tourism.

There are two major coffee plantations usually visited by tours: La Victoria and Buenavista. The latter was developed by French settlers

Coffee bean drying beds at an old coffee plantation

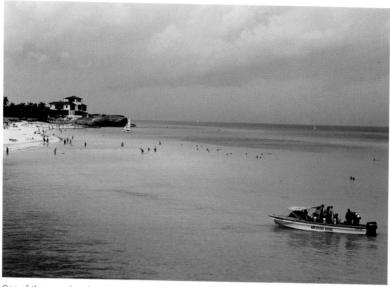

One of the many beaches along Varadero

escaping the Haiti Revolution in the 19th century. The colonial house has been restored, although the nearby slave barracks are in ruins.

The settlement at Las Terrazas was built in 1971 as a forestry and soil conservation station. Nearby slopes were terraced to prevent erosion and a large number of trees were planted to develop the area into an ecology reserve. As well as providing employment for local people, the area's sights attract a growing number of visitors. The Hotel Moka within the settlement is a beautiful Spanish colonial building, designed with ecological considerations in mind. There are bathing springs with cool, clear sulphur water nearby in the San Juan River, a delightful spot with small waterfalls, and deep pools surrounded by vegetation. There are changing facilities here too, so don't forget to take your bathing suit with you!

Varadero

Sitting on the 19km (11^1/$_2$-mile) Península de Hicacos, Cuba's most important beach resort for package holidays is also popular as a day excursion from Havana with tourists and locals alike. A typical day tour price will cost CUC35–64 and takes roughly ten hours.

The bus journey takes three hours. However, a full tour could be more convenient although a lot more expensive. For a full description of the resort, *see pp80 & 82.*

Western Cuba

Western Cuba is the area that most tourists focus on when they only have a limited amount of time in the country, after spending time in Havana and a beach resort such as Varadero. The area should not be missed, as it is one of outstanding natural beauty, with attractions and activities to suit a great variety of tastes.

The main attraction is the Viñales Valley, with an exotic landscape of limestone *mogotes* (outcrops), tobacco plantations, nature reserves, caves and mountains. In the far west, there is first-class scuba diving, as well as good beaches and ecotourist reserves.

The provincial towns and villages are quiet and agricultural, a far cry from the bustle of Havana, and the whole province offers a peaceful refuge from city sightseeing. It has always been a laid-back area, Pinar del Río province being known as the least

Province of Pinar del Río

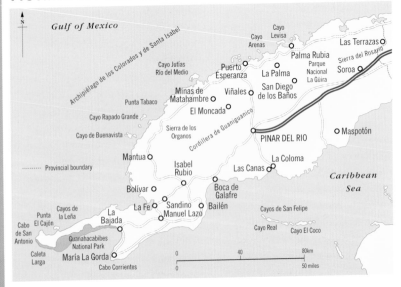

'revolutionary' part of Cuba. Pinar del Río is also the area that produces the best tobacco in Cuba, and therefore in the world.

PINAR DEL RÍO

The capital of the province is a lively and attractive town, and gives visitors a good taste of provincial Cuba. So named because of the many pine groves in the area, it has many neoclassical buildings with columns, as well as distinctive red tiles on the roofs of many houses.

Cigar factory

A visit to the cigar factory is included in most tours of the area. This tiny factory, which reputedly makes the best cigars in the world, is housed in a former 19th-century hospital, and visitors can watch workers sitting at desks, rolling leaves of dried tobacco and making *veguero* cigars, which are not exported.

Fábrica de Tabacos Francisco Donatién, Calle Maceo 157 Oeste. Open: Mon–Fri 9am–4pm and Sat 9am–noon. Admission charge if not part of a tour. Cameras and bags are not allowed in the factory.

Palacio de Guasch

A somewhat extravagant building, this has an unusual façade consisting of Moorish arches, Gothic spires and even baroque elements. It was built in 1909 for a wealthy physician who wanted to reproduce the architectural styles that inspired him during his travels.

Palacio de Guasch, Pinar del Río

Now the building is home to a natural history museum.

Calle Martí, corner of Comandante Pinares. Museum: Tel: 823087. Open: Tue–Sat 9am–5pm, Sun 9–11.30am. Admission charge.

THE SIERRA DEL ROSARIO

Now a UNESCO world biosphere reserve, the Sierra del Rosario mountain range covers the eastern part of Pinar del Río province, including a 250sq km (97sq mile) biosphere reserve.

Soroa

Please refer to the Soroa section within the Havana excursions chapter (*see pp70–72*).

81km (50 miles) southwest of Havana, in the Sierra del Rosario. Can be driven from the capital either directly from the autopista *(motorway) and driving northwest from Candelaria, or by going 18km (11 miles) west from Havana, then southeast from Moka through the Sierra del Rosario.*

Las Terrazas

Please refer to the Las Terrazas section in Havana excursions (*see pp72–3*).
51km (31 miles) west of Havana, and 4km (2¹/₂ miles) north of the autopista *(motorway), in the Sierra del Rosario.*

THE VIÑALES VALLEY

This valley, which has been declared a national monument, lies in the Sierra de los Organos and features huge limestone outcrops. It is worth at least a day's visit (a stay overnight in the area is recommended). Many tourist companies offer a tour of the valley which includes a visit to cigar and rum factories, and a tour of caves in the area.

Cueva del Indio

This beautiful cave was discovered in 1920. The first part of the tour here is on foot through tunnels, while a small motorboat takes visitors on the underground river (part of the San Vicente) through to the other side, about 0.5km (¹/₄ mile) away.

MOGOTES

Mogotes are limestone outcrops that resemble sugar loaves. They are some of the most ancient rocks in Cuba, and are the remains of what was once a limestone plateau. The soft limestone was eroded from the inside while hard limestone pillars remained with ancient caves within them. Although many have thick vegetation growing on them, there is often very little soil, with a number of endemic plant species growing here, including the corch palm and mountain palm tree.

6km (3¹/₂ miles) north of Viñales. Open: daily 9am–5pm. Try to avoid the rush between 11.30am and 2.30pm, when many tour parties visit. Admission charge when not part of a tour. Restaurant.

Gran Caverna de Santo Tomás

This is the largest network of caves in the whole of Latin America, with 18km (11 miles) of galleries and up to five levels of grottoes. In days gone by, the largest, the Cueva del Salón, was used by local farmers for festivals, but it is not normally open for tourists.
El Moncada, 17km (10¹/₂ miles) west of Viñales. Charge for cave walk and guide.

Mural de la Prehistoria

Although not to everyone's taste, this mural is on a grand scale, painted in 1962 on the face of a *mogote* by Lovigildo González, a pupil of the famous Mexican painter Diego Rivera. It depicts the history of evolution.
2km (1¹/₄ miles) west of Viñales, by the Mogote Dos Hermanos. Open: daily 8am–7pm. Admission charge.

Viñales

Although just a small town, Viñales is delightful and more pleasant to stay in than the much larger Pinar del Río. The town is now maintained by the government as an example of a well-preserved colonial settlement. The main street is lined with trees and wooden colonnades, and with red-tiled buildings typical of the area. The main square,

Torch ginger

Parque Martí, has been beautifully restored, as has the Iglesia del Sagrado Corazón de Jesús, which is now the home of the Casa de la Cultura, and includes an art gallery.

25km (15 miles) north of Pinar del Río in the Valle de Viñales. Nearby are two very good hotels: Hotel La Ermita and Hotel Los Jazmines.

THE WEST COAST

More effort is required to visit the Guanahacabibes Peninsula, which forms the western tip of Cuba, but it is well worth it if you are interested in either diving or nature. The peninsula was named after a pre-Columbian ethnic group. It consists of a strip of land 100km (60 miles) long and up to 34km (20½ miles) wide, and it was declared a world biosphere reserve in 1985, with the aim of protecting the flora and fauna.

Guanahacabibes National Park

A paradise for keen naturalists, the park contains 12 species of amphibian, 19 species of reptile including iguanas, 10 types of mammal, and 147 bird species, including woodpeckers, parrots and hummingbirds. There are fossil coastlines, caves and blue holes, while the forest is made up of a mix of deciduous and evergreen trees. The area is slowly gearing itself up to cater for ecotourists.

The park is at the far southwestern tip of Cuba. La Bajada is the nearby scientific station and community. Access to the inner zone is limited. Permits to enter can be obtained in Pinar del Río at tourist offices within hotels, and visits to the park are made in jeeps with a local guide.

María la Gorda

Reputedly the best diving centre in Cuba, María la Gorda is relatively isolated, but visitors will find beautiful coral reefs, warm translucent waters and a real tropical aquarium. The reefs are easy to reach, lying just a short distance from the shore. Areas of particular interest to divers include the Black Coral Valley, a wall of coral over 100m (328ft) long, and the Salón de María, a sea cave 18m (59ft) deep, which is home to rare species of fish.

The dive boat usually goes a short distance to dive sites, mostly reef or wall dives. Fish in the area include rays, turtles, reef and whale sharks, and barracuda. There is also good snorkelling, with small coral heads close to the white sand beach.

12km (7 miles) south of La Bajada. María la Gorda Diving Centre, La Bajada. Tel: 82-778131. Package tours can be arranged in Havana from Cubamar and Puertosol.

Cuban cigars

Cigars are integral to Cuba's culture and identity, and they are one of the country's abiding symbols. They are perhaps the most popular and sought-after souvenirs for tourists, and understandably so, because Cuba produces the finest cigars in the world. It is said that, just before he ordered the full trade embargo on Cuba in 1961, President Kennedy secretly ordered supplies of Cuban cigars to be bought for his personal use.

The origins of Cuban cigars begin with the native Indians who used tobacco (*cohiba*) during religious rites to invoke the gods. Columbus noted the natives' habit of smoking roughly rolled dried leaves during his second journey to the New World. The Spaniards soon acquired the taste for tobacco, and by the 17th century it was traded in the European market, being thought to have therapeutic qualities. Tobacco plantations were first established near the Río Almendares (now Havana), in the centre of the island, and later on in the west of the island. By the 19th century, tobacco planters and merchants were very prosperous.

Nowadays, tobacco is cultivated in the provinces of Pinar del Río, Villa Clara, Sancti Spíritus, Granma and Santiago de Cuba. It is a very labour-intensive process. Seedlings are transplanted from the nursery between October and December, and weeded after two weeks. Harvesting takes place from January to March, when the leaves are collected by hand, starting from the bottom of the plant. The leaves are hung up to dry until they turn yellow and then reddish-gold, which normally takes about 50 days. After the first fermentation of 30 days, the leaves are stripped of the main vein, dampened and packed for the second fermentation period of 60 days. Then, after a storage and ageing period of months or even years, they are rolled by teams of factory workers sitting at desks. A skilled factory worker makes an average of 120 cigars a day,

A *guajiro* (smallholder's cottage) amid fields of tobacco

A cigar maker at work

equipped with a *chaveta* knife, a guillotine and a pot of sap. *Torcedores* (cigar rollers) are highly skilled, often coming from generations of artisans.

Different types of leaves are used in the rolling of a cigar. The core of the cigar is made up of filler leaves, called *tripa*, which are chosen to obtain a particular flavour. Next is the *capote*, the binder leaf that keeps the core compact. Finally, the wrapper leaf (the *capa*) is rolled on the outside and gives the cigar its smooth, velvety appearance. After wrapping, the cigar is trimmed and then measured to gauge against various standard sizes in terms of length and diameter.

Cigars are made in different shapes and sizes. Heavy cigars tend to have a fuller flavour compared to standard or slim cigars, while some are tapered

(*figurado*). There are 32 brands of Cuban cigars, all of which have famous and often historic designs from the 19th century. Cohiba cigars have been produced for the international market since 1966 and tend to be the mildest, while Montecristo is one of the oldest brands, dating from 1935.

Care must be taken when buying cigars. Do not be tempted to buy them on the street, as these are likely to be low-quality fakes. Always buy from a state-run shop, and check that the box is sealed with a four-language warranty. On the bottom should be a stamp saying '*Habanos S.A. Hecho en Cuba totalmente a mano*'. The cigars should be tightly rolled, with no lumps, and nothing should come out if you turn them upside down.

Western Central Cuba

The Western Central region of Cuba consists of three provinces: Matanzas, Cienfuegos and Villa Clara. They are the rural heart of the island, with a gentle landscape and cultivated fields which you will see if travelling from Havana to Trinidad or further east. How much of this area tourists see depends very much on the time available to them.

Putting the famous holiday resort of Varadero to one side, there are the lively cities of Santa Clara and Cienfuegos, and to the south are the beautiful nature reserves in the Zapata Peninsula, a must for nature lovers.

From the mid-16th century, both coasts in this region were regularly raided by pirates for the best part of 200 years. Santa Clara was founded as a result of families moving inland, while Cienfuegos was founded 150 years later by settlers from the former French colonies of Haiti and Louisiana.

VARADERO

Cuba's chief beach resort has long been both popular and exclusive, illustrated by the fact that the 19km (11½ miles) Península de Hicacos on which the resort sits is connected to the mainland by a drawbridge. The only Cubans that tourists will meet in Varadero work in the tourist industry so it is all very safe, comfortable and sanitised. Staying in an all-inclusive resort in Varadero, wearing a coloured wristband, gives tourists zero exposure to the real Cuba.

Varadero is still undergoing large-scale development, mostly with foreign investors in joint ventures. Capacity is expected to reach 30,000 rooms, although it remains to be seen whether it becomes over-developed. Organised excursions are available for those wishing to see something of the rest of the country.

The peninsula is a succession of hotel villages with shops, cinemas, sports centres and nightlife venues. The southern end of the resort is more downmarket, while the northern end has more international-class luxury hotels. There is little of historical or architectural interest apart from a few tourist sites. The Museo Municipal recounts the history of Varadero, housed in a white and blue wooden chalet from the early 1900s. Villa Xanadu is a sumptuous mansion with golf course and gardens, built in 1929 by the American chemical engineer

Provinces of Matanzas, Villa Clara and Cienfuegos

Atlantic Ocean

JARDINES DEL REY

Cayo Santa María

Cayo Fragoso

Cayo Punta Arena

Caibarién

Remedios

Province of Villa Clara

Isabela de Sagua

Sagua la Grande

Santo Domingo

SANTA CLARA

Topes de Collantes

TRINIDAD

Corralillo

El Guea

Cardenás

Province of Matanzas

Jagüey Grande

Guamá

Aguada de Pasajeros

Ciego Montero

Province of Cienfuegos

CIENFUEGOS

Cumanayagua

El Nicho

Jagua

Varadero

MATANZAS

Valle de Yumurí

San Miguel de los Baños

Cuevas de Bellamar

Parque Nacional Península de Zapata

Playa Larga

Bahía de Cochinos

Playa Girón

Caleta Buena

Cayos Blancos del Sur

Caribbean Sea

Provincial boundaries

100km

50

60 miles

0

Alfred Dupont, and now houses the elegant Restaurante Las Américas. Nature lovers should visit Punta Hicacos, a nature reserve with some attractive features, and Parque Josone, a pretty park with a rowing lake.

PENÍNSULA DE ZAPATA

Visitors come to this area of Cuba for a number of specific reasons, making it different from other tourist centres on the island. The peninsula's main attractions include a wildlife park, excellent facilities for water sports and diving, and the Bay of Pigs invasion site.

The peninsula itself is one of the least populated on the island. It consists mostly of a huge swamp partly covered by forest, which forms one of the most complete wildlife reserves in the Caribbean. The area around Laguna del Tesoro has been designated a national park, the **Gran Parque Nacional de Montemar**, and it is the largest ecosystem on the island. Here one can walk among unspoilt nature and luxurious vegetation, look at mangroves, swamp plants, and birds with multicoloured plumage. For the more cautious tourist, do not worry; there are no poisonous snakes or other dangerous animals on the island!

Bahía de Cochinos

Bahía de Cochinos (Bay of Pigs) is in fact the name of the large bay, which includes a number of beaches and sights, including Playa Larga, Caleta de Rosario and Cueva de los Peces.

Península de Zapata

Visitors to the bay come mainly to visit the Bay of Pigs invasion site and for the excellent snorkelling and diving.

Playa Girón

Playa Girón is on the eastern side of the bay, and is home to the Museo Girón, which commemorates the famous battle which took place here in 1961.
Museo Girón, Playa Girón, Península de Zapata. Tel: 4122. Open: daily 9am– noon & 1–5pm. Admission charge.

Playa Larga

Playa Larga is a good base to explore the area and is also a popular resort with Cubans, as the beach is better than most along this part of the coast. Thick vegetation grows almost as far as the shore, although the resort area is better, with hotels and good facilities.

The coral reef offshore offers excellent dive sites. Around the bay to the east is Cueva de los Peces, a natural pool 70m (230ft) deep, full of fish and popular for diving and snorkelling.

Laguna del Tesoro

This 9sq km (3$\frac{1}{2}$sq mile) lagoon is over 10m (33ft) deep and an important home for flocks of migrating birds.

Criadero de Crocodilos

The crocodile farm is situated at the Zapata Tourist Institute, the biggest farm of its kind on the island. Founded in 1962, it safeguards 16 endangered species of reptile. Facilities are excellent.

BAY OF PIGS INVASION

Playa Girón is best known as the site of the decisive battle between Fidel Castro's revolutionary forces and the invading US-backed Cuban exiles, which took place at the height of the Cold War. On 17 April 1961, 1,400 Cuban exiles trained by the CIA landed on Cuban soil with the aim of overthrowing Castro's regime, supported by US Air Force planes, which bombed the island's air bases. They were met by Fidel Castro's forces as well as volunteers from the local population, which stopped the invasion in its tracks.

It was a controversial point in history, not only because it briefly threatened the newly born Cuban Revolution, but also because it was a humiliation for President Kennedy's presidency, and proved that the Revolution had won the hearts and minds of the Cuban people.

Open: daily 9am–4.30pm. Admission charge.

Villa Guamá

Situated in the middle of the lagoon, this is a replica Amerindian village where visitors can stay in wooden thatched huts with modern amenities such as air-conditioning. The huts are supported on stilts and are connected to one another by hanging bridges and canoes. This is an ideal place for birdwatchers, and the village has tourist facilities, including a restaurant, museum and even a disco! Insect repellent is recommended for staying overnight.
Boats are available to take you from Boca de Guamá to Villa Guamá for a fee. The journey takes one hour.

SANTA CLARA

Many tourists visit Santa Clara primarily to see the monumental Che Guevara mausoleum and sites related to the Cuban Revolution, in which Santa Clara played a decisive role. It is also used as a stopover city because it is central to the main tourist destinations on the island. While it is a pleasant university town, it does not have the same architectural history as Camagüey or Santiago de Cuba.

Santa Clara was founded in 1689 by people moving inland to escape pirate raids on the coast, but it was in 1958 that the town was made famous, when it gained its reputation as 'city of the heroic guerrilla'.

Memorial Comandante Ernesto Che Guevara

One of the most popular sites in the country for Cubans to visit, this monument in the Plaza de la Revolución was built in 1988 to commemorate the 30th anniversary of the battle of Santa Clara. The memorial

Monument to Che Guevara

is dominated by the famous bronze statue of Che with his arm in plaster (he had broken it during the battle). Under the monument is a mausoleum and the **Museo Histórico de la Revolución**, which has some of Che's personal belongings on display. *Plaza de la Revolución Ernesto Che Guevara. Open: Tue–Sun 9am–5pm. Free admission.*

BATTLE OF SANTA CLARA

In December 1958 Che Guevara's forces had already defeated government forces to gain control of the city the day before, when dictator Batista sent an armoured train with soldiers and supplies to reinforce Santiago de Cuba. Guevara and his limited number of men ambushed the train, causing the surrender of the troops, a decisive battle which led to Batista fleeing the country. The remains of Che Guevara are interred in the mausoleum at the site of his greatest victory.

Monumento a la Toma del Tren Blindado

The historic ambush of Batista's troop train is commemorated in this museum-monument, on the spot where it took place. Four carriages have been preserved, as well as the bulldozer used to cause the derailment of the train, and other memorabilia. Overlooking the site is the hill El Capiro, where Che and his troops waited for the train. There are excellent views from here over the city. *Open Mon–Sat 9am–5.30pm. Admission charge.*

Parque Leoncio Vidal

This charming park is in the heart of the city with flower beds, wrought-iron benches and period street lamps from the 1920s. The plaza's charm makes it a popular place for residents to stroll, both day and night, and some of the buildings around the square have been renovated. The park was named after the colonel in the national independence army who was killed in battle in the square in 1896.

Until 1894, the square was racially segregated, with blacks having to walk around the outside areas of the park.

Between Calles Marta Abreu, Colón and Cuba.

Teatro La Caridad

The austere exterior of this late 19th-century theatre belies the beautifully ornate interior, which has painted panels and chandeliers. The name 'La Caridad' (charity) came from the offering of additional services such as a restaurant, barber, ballroom and gambling, which collected money for the poor of the city. The theatre itself is most interesting, with wrought-iron balusters and some folding seats (an innovation in Cuba at the time), as well as a beautifully frescoed ceiling by the Spanish artist Camilo Salaya. *Parque Vidal 3. Tel: 205548.*

Western Central Cuba

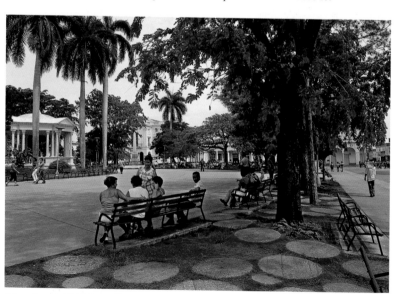

Parque Leoncio Vidal, Santa Clara

Che Guevara

Without doubt, Che Guevara is the Cuban Revolution's greatest hero and his iconic status is due perhaps as much to his photogenic looks and charismatic personality as to his extraordinary leadership qualities and courage in the field of battle. He believed in a revolutionary society based on moral rather than material wealth, and defended Third World rights with great eloquence.

The enigmatic Che Guevara

Ernesto Guevara was born in Argentina, acquiring the nickname 'Che' after an Argentinian figure of speech. Initially a medical student, he started his personal struggle against imperialism in Guatemala at the time when the CIA toppled the elected government, and he met Fidel Castro in Mexico soon afterwards. He joined Fidel's group of rebels in the run-up to the guerrilla struggle against Batista's dictatorship, and was a key commander in the military success of the Revolution in 1959. His greatest moment was the capture of Santa Clara and the successful ambush, in December 1958, of Batista's troop and munitions train. This subsequently resulted in Batista fleeing the country and victory for the revolution. Guevara took the position of head of the Central Bank and the Ministry of Industry, overseeing a period of chaotic economic reforms.

Guevara's role in the new government was not successful and he became disillusioned, leaving for the Congo and then Bolivia to join the guerrilla struggles there. In 1967 he was captured by CIA-backed government troops and executed in Bolivia.

In 1997, on the 30th anniversary of his death, the body of Che Guevara was returned to Cuba and interred in a bronze mausoleum in Santa Clara. He remains one of only two foreigners in the history of the island to be proclaimed a Cuban citizen 'by birth'; the other was Dominican Máximo Gómez, the general in the Wars of Independence.

KORDA'S PHOTO

Alberto Díaz Gutiérrez could never have imagined that one of the magazine photos that he took of Che Guevara, rejected by the newspaper *Revolución*, would become so famous.

The son of a railway worker, the young fashion photographer took the name 'Korda' because he thought that it sounded like 'Kodak' and would therefore be better for business. When he was 31, an expedition into the countryside showed him the reality of peasant life with its grinding poverty; he became a revolutionary, and photographer for the revolutionary leadership. His famous photograph of Che was taken in 1960 at the funeral of a Cuban merchant seaman killed in a sabotaged munitions ship.

A huge poster of the photo was used as a backdrop for Fidel Castro's speech in Plaza de la Revolución that paid homage to Che upon his death in 1967. The global coverage of the event catapulted the image, and Che, to iconic status. It has subsequently been used on everything from T-shirts and posters to advertisements.

The photo was used without permission, and Korda did nothing about his copyright or possible royalties for ten years. It was only in 1998 that Korda sued and won damages following the use of the photo in yet another advertising campaign. He donated the money to the Cuban health service because he believed that Che would have done the same.

Korda died in 2001 at the age of 73.

CIENFUEGOS

Despite being surrounded by industry and unspectacular scenery, the maritime town of Cienfuegos has a well-preserved charm and some fascinating architectural gems, as well as a captivating bay. While it is a historic town, it also has a well-to-do feel to it. Well worth visiting on the outskirts are the magnificent botanical gardens and the aquarium, which are often on the itinerary of tour buses to Cienfuegos.

The small province of Cienfuegos is largely low-lying, with an emphasis on sugar plantations, sugar being the mainstay for the town's wealth, along with cattle. The diving is also good along the coast.

Founded in 1819, the town was named after the first Cuban Governor General at the time, José Cienfuegos. As one of the few towns in Cuba founded by the French rather than the Spanish, it has an interesting blend of architectural styles. The town was planned in a geometric layout following neoclassical guidelines. In the colonial era, it was named 'pearl of the south', due to the beauty of the town and bay. There are many legends here about pirates, and the fortress was built by the Spanish in 1745 as a result of the threat of attack.

The town centre

Cienfuegos has a comfortable, relaxed atmosphere, partly due to the bustle in the streets, especially the pedestrianised main shopping street (Avenida 54, known as the Boulevard), which seems to have more shops than in other Cuban towns.

The other main street in the town is Paseo del Prado (Calle 37), which has a central promenade for people to stroll along or sit. It is the liveliest thoroughfare in the city, established in 1922, flanked by elegant, well-

Avoiding the midday sun in Cienfuegos

The Paseo del Prado, the main thoroughfare in Cienfuegos

preserved buildings, with monuments in the centre honouring the great and the good.

Catedral de la Purísima Concepción

One of the major buildings around Parque Martí is the Cathedral of Cienfuegos, with two bell towers of different heights, and a neoclassical façade. Built in 1869, it has stained-glass windows made in France and a neo-Gothic interior with silvered columns.
Avenida 56, on the east side of Calle 29. Tel: 515297. Open: Mon–Fri 7am–3pm, Sat 7am–noon & 2–4pm, Sun 7am–noon.

Museo Provincial

Formerly the casino, this eclectic-style building opened in 1896. Now the Provincial Museum, it houses period objects and furniture reflecting the great wealth of the leading families of the area in the 19th century. There are also two rooms of contemporary art.
South side of Parque Martí, on Avenida 54. Tel: 519722. Open: Tue–Sat 10am–6pm, Sun 9am–1pm. Admission charge.

Palacio de Ferrer

This is a beautiful early 19th-century building of eclectic architecture, with a distinctive cupola, situated on the west side of Parque Martí. Although the interior is sadly neglected, it still has impressive marble floors, staircases and walls, and Italian ceramic wall tiles, that hint at the grandeur of past times.

There are some rusty spiral steps going up to the tower for some great views of the area. It is now the **Casa de Cultura Benjamín Duarte**, but was originally built by the sugar magnate José Ferrer. *Avenida 54, corner of Calle 25, on the west side of Parque Martí. Tel: 516584. Open: Mon–Sat 8.30am–7pm. Voluntary admission charge.*

Palacio de Valle

Normally included in city tours, this is the most striking and original building for miles around. Now a restaurant, it is almost obscenely lavish in its decoration. The palace was built in 1917 by one of the wealthiest men in Cuba at the time, the sugar merchant Acisclo del Valle Blanco, and subsequently became a casino in dictator Batista's time.

The two-storey building is decorated with Gothic, Venetian and neo-Moorish styles and was inspired by the owner's travels in Europe, especially by the Moorish architecture of southern Spain. *Calle 37 between Avenida 0 and 2, Punta Gorda. Tel: 511226. Open: daily 9.30am–11pm. Admission charge.*

Parque Martí

Formerly the Plaza de Armas, this square is vast, with many buildings of historical importance surrounding it. As a result, it has been declared a national monument. It was here in 1819 that the city was founded in a solemn ceremony under a hibiscus tree. In the middle of the park is the 'zero kilometre', the central point marking the middle of Cienfuegos. It is a very pleasant park, with a rotunda bandstand, benches and a statue of José Martí at one end. The arch on the west side of the square is the only triumphal arch in Cuba, symbolising the entrance to the city, and was commissioned in 1902 by the workers' corporation. One side of the square is taken up by the provincial government assembly building, the Palacio del Ayuntamiento. The buildings around the square are mostly in an excellent state of repair, making it a popular stopping point for tours.

Teatro Tomás Terry

A masterpiece of 19th-century architecture, this theatre was built in 1889 to fulfil the last will of the Venezuelan sugar magnate and former mayor Tomás Terry Adams, with the proceeds of a donation by his family. The Italian-style building is a beautifully preserved, charming two-tiered auditorium. There is a lovely fresco by Camilo Salaya, a Spanish painter, and world-famous performers such as Enrico Caruso and Sarah Bernhardt performed here in the 1900s. Two sets of theatre boxes nearest the stage were traditionally reserved for mourners who did not want to be seen by the rest of the audience, and who could enter and leave the theatre through a separate door. *Avenida 56 (San Carlos), overlooking Parque Martí. Tel: 513361. Open: daily*

9am–6pm. Admission charge includes guided tour. Extra charge for taking photos.

Out of town
Castillo de Jagua

This majestic military structure was the third most important fortress on the island in the 18th century. It served the important purpose of protecting the region from Jamaican pirates. Legend has it that a mysterious lady ghost used to walk the corridors of the citadel every night, frightening the guards.

The fortress currently includes a restaurant that specialises in fish dishes.
Poblado Castillo de Jagua, 29km (18 miles) south of the town. Ferries to the fortress available from Avenida 46 amd Calle 25 in Cienfuegos harbour. Open: daily 8am–5pm. Admission charge.

Jardín Botánico de Cienfuegos

Outside of Cienfuegos, but well worth a special trip or detour, is the city's botanical garden, which is one of the largest in Latin America at 90 hectares (222 acres), and which is now a national monument. It is also known as Jardín Botánico Soledad, named after the sugar mill built by the garden's founder, Edwin Atkins. It has more than 2,000 different species of plant, including 300 types of palm trees. Of special interest are a gigantic Banyan tree with aerial roots and a circumference of over 20m (66ft), and the many examples of cacti in the greenhouse.
23km (14 miles) east of Cienfuegos, between the villages of San Antón and Los Guaos. Open: daily 8am–5pm. Admission charge. Guides are only in Spanish; tips are welcomed.

The extravagant Palacio de Valle

TRINIDAD

Arriving in Trinidad is like stepping into a time warp that takes you back to colonial times. The perfectly preserved buildings and cobbled streets result from the town's isolation from the rest of Cuba for 100 years, and its status as a UNESCO World Heritage Site. Sections of the town have been skilfully restored.

The city was founded in 1514 by Diego Velázquez, and was a major trade centre in the 17th and 18th centuries, especially in sugar and slaves. Many of the town's museums are housed in the old residences of the landowners of this time.

By the mid-19th century, Trinidad went into decline, mainly because of the Industrial Revolution in Europe

Trinidad

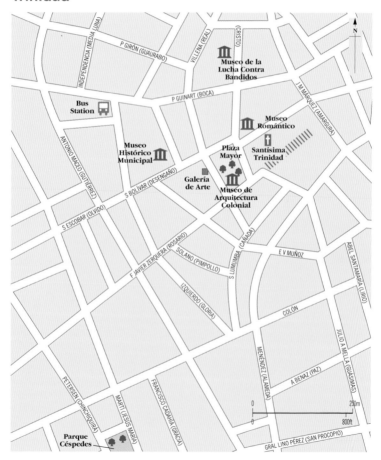

Museo de la Lucha Contra Bandidos

P GIRÓN (GUAURABO)

INDEPENDENCIA (MEDIA LUNA)

VILLENA (REAL)

(CRISTO)

J M MÁRQUEZ (AMARGURA)

P GUINART (BOCA)

Bus Station

Museo Romántico

ANTONIO MACEO (GUTIÉRREZ)

Museo Histórico Municipal

Plaza Mayor

Santísima Trinidad

Galería de Arte

Museo de Arquitectura Colonial

S BOLÍVAR (DESENGAÑO)

S ESCOBAR (OLVIDO)

F JAVIER ZERQUERA (ROSARIO)

SOLANO (PIMPOLLO)

S LUMUMBA (CAÑADA)

E V MUÑOZ

ABEL SANTAMARÍA (LIRIO)

IZQUIERDO (GLORIA)

COLÓN

JULIO A MELLA (GUASIMAS)

MENÉNDEZ (ALAMEDA)

A BENAZ (PAZ)

PETERSEN (CHINCHURRA)

MARTÍ (JESÚS MARÍA)

FRANCISCO CADAHÍA (GRACIA)

Parque Céspedes

GRAL LINO PÉREZ (SAN PROCOPIO)

0   250m
0   800ft

which powered the production of sugar beet. As a result, Trinidad became frozen in time until the 1950s.

Trinidad is a quaint, easy-going town with cobblestone streets and pastel-coloured houses, and worth at least two days' stay. It is also an ideal base from which to visit nearby towns, and for exploring the picturesque countryside of rolling hills, waterfalls and beaches.

STREET NAMES IN TRINIDAD

The names of Trinidad's streets are confusing, as each has an old name and a new one, pre- and post-Cuban Revolution. The old ones have been painted over in white but are still legible. There is some debate among locals as to which they prefer; many like the old names, although it would be inappropriate to speak against the new revolutionary names in public.

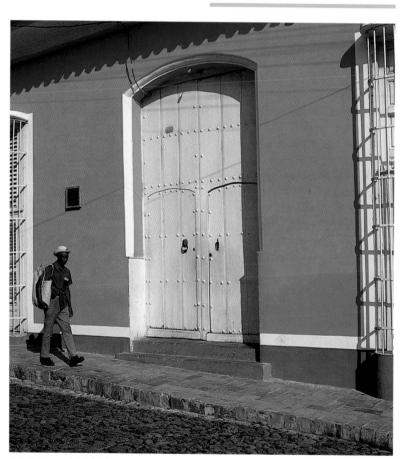

Colonial house in Trinidad

Plaza Mayor, Trinidad

Plaza Mayor lies at the heart of the town, and many of the principal museums and buildings face this square, making it easy to see most of the city's sights in a day. The benches in the square are a perfect place to relax in the shade of the palms and watch the colourful buildings around you change hue as the sun loses its strength in the late afternoon.

Iglesia y Convento de San Francisco

One block north of Plaza Mayor lies this monastery, symbol of the town, with fine views from its bell tower. The building was originally used by Franciscan monks in 1813, but it has subsequently been used as a garrison for the Spanish army, a school, and is now home to the **Museo de la Lucha Contra Bandidos**, exhibiting photos and memorabilia from the campaign against counter-revolutionaries in the Escambray Mountains in the 1960s.
Calle Echerri, corner of Guinart. Tel: 4121. Open: Mon–Sat 9am–5pm, Sun 9am–1pm. Admission charge.

Iglesia Parroquial Mayor de la Santísima Trinidad

This is the largest church in Cuba, dominating the Plaza Mayor. Famous for its acoustics, the highlights of this late 19th-century church are the beautiful carved wooden altars made of precious woods. Also impressive is the statue of Señor de la Vera Cruz ('Lord of the True Cross'); made in Spain and intended for Mexico, its journey was disrupted three times by strong winds that blew the ship back to Trinidad. The decision to leave part of the cargo behind, including the statue, was seen as a sign from heaven, and the statue has been worshipped since then. Christ of the True Cross is the patron of Trinidad.
East side of Plaza Mayor. Open: Mon–Sat 10.30am–1pm. Mass Sun at 9am.

Museo de Arquitectura Colonial

This pretty colonial mansion on the southeast of the square is the only museum of its kind in Cuba, covering different architectural styles in the town and illustrating colonial building techniques. The building was the

A 19th-century shower in the Museo de Arquitectura Colonial

Plaza Mayor with Palacio Brunet

residence of the Sánchez Iznaga family in the 18th century, who made their money from sugar. It has slim columns, wooden beams and a pretty portico, and one of the highlights is a 19th-century version of a shower with an array of pipes for hot and cold water. *Southeast side of Plaza Mayor. Tel: 3208. Open: Mon–Thur, Sat 9am–5pm, Sun 9am–1pm. Admission charge.*

Palacio Brunet (**Museo Romántico**)

Perhaps the most attractive museum in the town, the Museo Romántico has an impressive collection of ornaments, furniture and paintings in the Romantic style. The objects complement the building well, which was owned, as always in Trinidad, by a wealthy local businessman, in this case the Conde de Brunet, who lived in the house with his family in the mid-19th century and made his fortune from slaves and sugar. When he died, his properties included

two sugar mills and 700 slaves. Locals often use the Museo Romántico as a setting for wedding photos. *Northern corner of Plaza Mayor, next to the church of Santísima Trinidad. Tel: 4363. Open: Tue–Sat 9am–5pm, Sun 9am–1pm. Admission charge, plus charge for taking photos.*

Palacio Cantero (**Museo Histórico Municipal**)

As well as having a commanding view of the historic town centre, this museum also exhibits items recounting the history of the region with historical, cultural and scientific displays. The sumptuous 19th-century building is neoclassical in style, and the frescoed entrance hall, in particular, is beautiful, making the museum popular with tour parties. *Calle Bolívar 423. Tel: 4460. Open: daily 9am–5pm. Admission charge.*

Walk: Plaza Mayor, Trinidad

The area around Plaza Mayor is so small that a tour will not involve much walking – instead, the effort will be in absorbing the history of Trinidad and avoiding tripping up on the cobblestones, which are uneven. Thankfully the pavements are flat!

Allow 2 hours.

Although relatively short, you may find this walk tiring due to the heat of the sun. Keep in the shade as much as possible and remember to take regular breaks for drinks at the bars dotted around the square! For example, there is the Casa de la Música up the steps on the right-hand side of the Iglesia Parroquial de la Santísima Trinidad, and there is often a band playing there to keep you entertained. The logical starting point for the walk is in Plaza Mayor, under the shade of the palm trees.

1 Museo de Arquitectura Colonial

This first port of call offers an introduction to the architecture of Trinidad. The Casa de los Sánchez Iznaga, which houses the museum, is also a beautiful example of the kind of restoration that is typical in Trinidad.
Walk downhill across the square, past the yellow Casa de Aldemán Ortiz, turn left and walk one block down Bolívar. The entrance to the Museo Histórico is just after Calle Toro.

2 Palacio Cantero

Now the Museo Histórico, this is worth a visit not only for the exhibits on the history of the region, but also for the great views to be had from the tower.
Walk back uphill on Bolívar, and take a left along Villena.

3 Plazuela del Jigüe

This tiny area in front of the El Jigüe restaurant is where the first Mass in Trinidad was celebrated in 1514, beneath the acacia (*jigüe*) tree. Notice the lovely painted tiles on the outside of the porticoed restaurant.
Just up from this square is a pale green building with a few steps up to the door.

4 La Canchánchara

A quaint *casa de infusiones* with lovely shaded tables outside, this *casa* is famous for the cocktail of the same name, made with rum, sugar, honey, lime and water, and served in an earthenware pot. An ideal spot to

sample a refreshing *canchánchara* and listen to traditional music.
Once out of the building, turn left and left again, walking uphill on Guinart to the corner and then left on Cristo.

5 Iglesia y Convento de San Francisco

The church bell tower is the symbol of the city and offers fine views of the town. This monastery is home to the Museo de la Lucha Contra Bandidos.
Walk back towards Plaza Mayor along Echerri and look for the ochre building on your left.

6 Museo Romántico

The museum, housed in Palacio Brunet, has an impressive collection of furniture and other items that belonged to the Brunet family. It is easy to imagine the lifestyle of wealthy local families.
Further along Echerri is the church.

7 Iglesia Parroquial de la Santísima Trinidad

Built in the late 19th century, the Church of the Holy Trinity has a beautiful carved wooden altar and is the largest church in Cuba.

Other Trinidad sights

Ermita de Nuestra Señora de la Candelaria de la Popa

Visitors wanting a view of the city from the nearby hill will walk past this small church via a narrow, steep street from Plaza Mayor. Although closed, it is in a beautiful location. Damaged by a cyclone in 1812, the three-arch bell tower was added later. The walk further uphill takes you to a television transmission tower from which there are great views across the area.

Motel Las Cuevas

This hillside motel has two swimming pools, which are open to non-residents, as well as other facilities and shops. It is an ideal place to come for a swim, when sightseeing in hot weather is taking its toll. It has wonderful views and a relaxed atmosphere. Nearby is the motel disco, which is housed in a cave, and which plays mostly salsa and *merengue* dance music.

Trinidad excursions

The main attractions outside Trinidad are the beautiful scenery of the Sierra del Escambray, which includes the Topes de Collantes and Valle de los Ingenios, and nearby beaches. These can either be visited by booking tours at a tourist desk (Cubatour, Rumbos or Cubanacán are the main ones in Trinidad), or by taking a taxi, which will cost roughly the same as a tour if there are more than two people in your party.

Playa Ancón

About 10km (6 miles) south of Trinidad, this is the best beach resort in the area, with white sand and clean, turquoise water. The best part of the beach is in front of Hotel Ancón, which offers boat excursions for snorkelling and diving. It is a pleasant day trip from the town, but it should be mentioned that the beach is not quite up to the standard of those on the north coast.

10km (6 miles) south of Trinidad. Irregular bus services from Trinidad, although taxis and 'coco' taxis are always available in town to take you there for a few dollars.

Topes de Collantes

The most popular excursion from Trinidad takes you to the Parque Natural Topes de Collantes, offering lovely scenery in the unspoilt landscape of the Sierra del Escambray. There are several paths in the area offering stunning views of the lush forest and the opportunity to see wildlife such as butterflies, hummingbirds and even the *tocororo*, the national bird of Cuba, whose colours are reflected in the national flag.

At 800m (2,625ft) above sea level, and with good clean air, the area was the site of a sanitarium for lung diseases, and it is now an anti-stress centre and hotel.

The most popular trek takes you on a downward two-hour hike through the forest, passing curious rock formations, until you reach the Salto del Caburní, a steep, plunging waterfall that gushes over rocks and collects in a lovely pool. Many people take their swimming costumes for a refreshing swim in the cool water, which is also just the thing to prepare you for the steep climb back up!

The Topes de Collantes

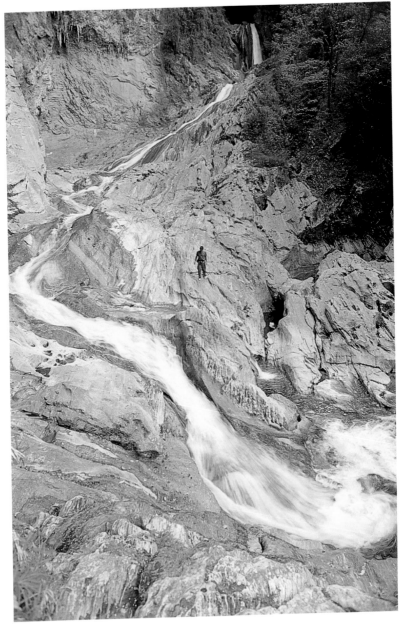

The Salto del Caburní waterfall

A day tour by jeep is the most convenient way to visit the area, as the 30-minute drive north of Trinidad is steep and four-wheel drives are necessary to take you right to the start of the trek. A hire car or taxi will be unsuitable for the last part of the journey. Tours will often include a knowledgeable guide to describe the huge range of endemic species of flora and fauna, some with weird and wonderful features. Remember to wear strong shoes, as the walk is steep and rocky. Don't attempt the trek if it has been raining, as this makes the tracks slippery and highly dangerous.

Torre de Manaca Iznaga and Valle de los Ingenios

This valley is only 12km (7½ miles) from Trinidad, and is rich in history that reflects its importance as a producer of sugar in the 19th century. UNESCO has declared the valley a World Heritage Site as a result. The word *ingenios* means 'sugar mills'.

One way of seeing the valley is to take the steam train that leaves Trinidad daily and covers the entire valley. The railroad was built in 1919 because of its importance in transporting sugar cane. Cuba was in fact the first country in the Americas to build a railway. The railway takes one hour to reach the Manaca Iznaga Estate, where 350 slaves worked in the 1840s. The landowner's house now includes a restaurant and shops, but the main attraction is the tower, which gives impressive views over the surrounding countryside.

It consists of seven levels, the first three square in shape, the top four octagonal, totalling a height of 45m (147ft). At the foot of the tower is the bell that tolled the work hours on the plantation and also alerted the ranchers to an escaped slave.

Trains leave Trinidad at 9.30am daily for an excursion of 5 hours. It is best to check with the rail station first (Calle Bolívar 422; tel: 3348) or a tourist desk. The station is about 15 minutes' walk from the town centre. Please note that trains returning to Trinidad are irregular, which may mean that you are killing time at Manaca Iznaga waiting for the return train, once you have visited the tower (admission charge). The alternative to the train is a taxi from the town centre which may be more convenient, especially if there are two or more of you.

SUGAR PLANTATIONS

Sugar has been the basis for Cuba's economy throughout its history. French sugar planters came to Cuba to escape the Haiti revolution, and brought their expertise with them. With the growing demand in Europe and America, large numbers of slaves needed to be imported from 1793 onwards to work in the sugar plantations and factories. Cuba became a plantation society, and was the biggest exporter of sugar in the world, with 1 million slaves accounting for more than half the population. This led to the emergence of sugar factories (*ingenios*), slave barracks (*barracones*), and religion, music and dance specific to the slave culture. For example, rumba music is thought to have developed from this culture.

Eastern Central Cuba

While Trinidad is the main attraction in this part of Cuba, there is much else to do and see, including excellent diving and swimming, and visits to other colonial towns. The provinces here are Sancti Spíritus, Ciego de Ávila, Camagüey, Holguín and Las Tunas; many have not seen much tourist development, but the countryside is pretty, with swathes of sugar cane, hillsides with thatched cottages, palm trees, and lovely bays and beaches, protected by coral reefs. Columbus himself stated that it was the most beautiful country he had ever seen.

It is easy to regard the towns in this area simply as transit towns that break up the journey between Havana, Trinidad and Santiago de Cuba, but they have an atmosphere of their own, vibrant and authentically Cuban.

For example, Sancti Spíritus is an attractive colonial town and is one of the oldest towns on the island, being founded in 1514. It receives few visitors despite its status as a National Monument. The capital of the province, it suffers from its proximity to Trinidad, its colonial charm not matching its rival's well-preserved beauty.

Ciego de Ávila, on the other hand, is a more modern town, only becoming a city in 1840. Also a provincial capital, it has little of architectural interest, and the visitors it has are mostly on their way to the popular diving sites in the Jardines de la Reina archipelago. The province of Ciego de Ávila is also famous for activities such as freshwater fishing and game shooting.

Las Tunas province, a small agricultural province, is often forgotten by tourists. The capital is an unpretentious and pleasant transit town, but the main draws are the lovely beaches. The province has 35 virgin beaches, the most popular understandably being Playa Covarrubias with a 3km (2-mile) coral reef and fine white sand.

CAMAGÜEY

The province of Camagüey is the largest in Cuba, with flat but pretty countryside. Its colonial capital city has a distinctly Cuban feel to it, unlike the tourist towns of Havana and Trinidad. However, restoration is being carried out on old buildings and squares, and there is much to see, particularly concerning the revolutionary history of the 19th and 20th centuries. Saturday nights are lively in the town, with street parties and a busy throng of Cubans, young and old, enjoying the cool evening breeze in the squares and on the streets.

Camagüey is nicknamed 'the Legendary', on account of its traditions of heroism and patriotism. Several key figures are commemorated in the town, including Ignacio Agramonte, who was killed in action in 1873. Originally founded on the coast and gaining prosperity mainly through livestock and then sugar, the city was moved inland to escape pirate attacks.

Casa Natal de Ignacio Agramonte

This pretty two-storey house from 1750 was the former home of one of the national heroes in the struggle against Spanish colonialism. Ignacio Agramonte was born in the house in 1841, becoming a lawyer and cattle rancher before leading a rebellion in the area against the Spanish. He died in 1873 after being wounded in action. The top floor of the house is a museum displaying the patriot's personal belongings, while the beautiful courtyard is used for concerts (note the old *tinajones* (clay jars) lying here). *459 Calle Ignacio Agramonte, opposite the church on Plaza de los Trabajadores. Tel: 297116. Open: Tue–Sat 9am–5pm, Sun 9am–11.30pm. Admission charge.*

Catedral de Nuestra Señora de la Candelaria

The town's cathedral is on the south side of the park, and, along with the square itself, has undergone several restorations. It is dedicated to Our Lady of Candelaria, the patron saint of the

Eastern Central provinces

The post office in Camagüey

city. It was originally built in the early 18th century, but reconstructed in 1864, giving it its present-day appearance. *Calle Independencia 64, Parque Agramonte. Open: Mon–Fri 8.30am–noon & 2–6pm, Sun 8–11am. Mirador (viewing point). Admission charge.*

Museo Ignacio Agramonte

The prestigious art collection in this museum is said to be second only to that in the Museo de Bellas Artes in Havana, including works by the famous Cuban artist Fidelio Ponce (1895–1949), who was born in Camagüey. This was the only military building in town, being the headquarters of the Spanish army cavalry in the latter half of the 19th century. The museum was inaugurated in 1955 and includes exhibits on history, natural history, archaeology, and the art of the province. *Avenida de los Mártires 2. Tel: 282425. Open: Tue–Thur, Sat 10am–6pm, Fri noon–8pm, Sun 9am–1pm. Admission charge.*

Nuestra Señora de la Merced

The main attraction in this church is the Santo Sepulcro, a silver coffin, constructed in 1762 with the donation of 23,000 silver coins. Before the Revolution, it used to be carried in procession along the town streets.

The church was originally built in 1601, but rebuilt in 1756, resulting in a baroque façade with a central bell tower. The interior has some striking murals that are almost art nouveau in style. A cemetery was on the original site of the church, and the catacombs can still be seen, including some bones and skulls. In the courtyard there are 19th-century cannons abandoned by the Spanish. The external clock on the church was the first public clock in the town. The church is slowly being restored.

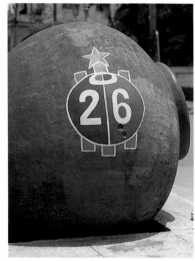

A *tinajón* (clay jar)

Plaza de los Trabajadores 4. Tel: 292783. Open: Mon–Sat 8–11am & 3–5pm, Sun 8–10am & 4.30–6pm. Free admission.

CAMAGÜEY'S PECULIARITIES

Despite the town being moved inland in the 17th century, it was still attacked by pirates, including the Welshman Henry Morgan. Architects began to design the town with narrow, irregular street networks, in order to confuse and deter attackers. It is a town layout that makes it very awkward to find your way around, so a good map is recommended.

Another peculiarity of Camagüey is the *tinajones*, which have become symbols of the city. These large jars are found everywhere, especially in the courtyards of colonial houses and in parks. They are made of clay from the nearby hills, and some can be as large as 2m (6½ft) in height. The jars were introduced by Catalonian immigrants in the early 1700s, and are still used today to collect rainwater and to store food.

Parque Ignacio Agramonte

The main square in the town, this was initially the Plaza de Armas. It is a beautiful square with marble paving, clean and very well restored. It is a hub for locals, especially in the evenings when residents of all ages come to sit around the square, enjoying the tranquil atmosphere and listening to musicians. The equestrian statue in the middle of the square is of the local independence hero Ignacio Agramonte, who died in battle in 1873. Royal palms stand at the four corners of the square in memory of a group of nationalists executed here in 1851.

Flamingoes in a Cayo Coco hotel garden

CAYO COCO

Although isolated from the rest of Cuba, Cayo Coco attracts a large number of tourists who stay here mostly on package holidays, but do not venture very far. For those interested in crystal-clear waters, fine white sand and warm water, Cayo Coco is idyllic. Other attractions include some of the best ecotourist facilities in Cuba, with a natural reserve for marine birds.

Cayo Coco has become a focal point in the government's drive to develop Cuba as an ecotourist destination. Plans include a rapid expansion in large, luxury resorts, all built and operated by foreign businesses. The island of Cayo Coco, or the *coco*, as Cubans refer to it, is 374sq km (144sq miles) in size, connected to the mainland just north of Morón by a 27km (17-mile) causeway. It has 22km (14 miles) of sandy beaches, with the remaining land being partly marshy, abundant in mangroves and coconut palms.

Parador la Silla

The ideal spot for viewing flamingoes, which flock here between April and November to breed.
On the end of the causeway furthest away from the Cuban mainland.

Playa Los Flamencos

Perhaps one of the best beaches on the island, Playa Los Flamencos is renowned for its clear, shallow waters and white sand, extending for 5km (3 miles). Flamingoes, after which the beach is named, can be seen all year round. There are now about 35,000 birds in the cays (islands).
Near the northern tip of Cayo Coco island. 15 minutes' drive from hotels: most people take tours from the various hotels here.

Playa Prohibida

Anyone looking for peace and seclusion need look no further. This beach is appropriately named, since the government has banned construction here in order to protect the environment. There is a nature trail which starts nearby and leads to the centre of Cayo Coco, and the beach itself is surrounded by large dunes, some rising as high as 40m (131ft).
Just a few miles west of the village of Güira.

CAYO GUILLERMO

This small island specialises in fishing. Ernest Hemingway was a dedicated fan of the area and praised it in his book *Islands in the Stream*. The cay is protected by a long coral reef which is good for diving. The beach is 5km (3 miles) long, with some of the highest sand dunes in the area, covered in mangroves, palms and other trees such as mahogany and juniper.

Northwest of Cayo Coco island, linked to it by a causeway.

An idyllic beach at Cayo Coco

View of the bay from Gibara Hill

BAHÍA DE BARIAY AND GUARDALAVACA

While Bahía de Bariay and Guardalavaca are more than 30km (19 miles) apart, visitors to the area are unlikely to see one and not the other. They are both highly recommended to tourists, but for different reasons. The first is a historically important site just off the colonial town of Gibara, while the latter is a mecca for sun-worshipping resort tourists.

Bahía de Bariay

Great views of this bay can be had by hiking up El Cuartelón (El Mirador). Most historians agree that Columbus landed here on 28 October 1492, on a spit of land in the middle of a bay (Cayo de Bariay), and was astounded by the beauty of the area. There is a monument here marking the 500th anniversary of his landing, called *Encuentro* (encounter), which is dedicated to the Taíno Indians. The pretty town of Gibara has higgledy-piggledy deep-red tiled roofs; it was founded in 1817 and is still important for fishing.

Bahía de Bariay lies east of Gibara town, about 32km (20 miles) north of Holguín. The monument is relatively remote if travelling by car, but boat trips can be arranged from Guardalavaca.

Guardalavaca

The beach resort of Guardalavaca is the second most popular in Cuba, after Varadero, and is on a beautiful stretch of coastline, indented with horseshoe bays. It is famous for its lovely clear turquoise sea, fine sand and coral reefs close to the shore.

Although it is within easy reach of Holguín (58km/36 miles), it still feels slightly isolated. The area has been extensively developed since the 1980s and is now a popular tourist resort. The name Guardalavaca literally means 'watch the cow', a Spanish term used for the cattle egret, a very common bird in this part of Cuba.

COLUMBUS IN CUBA

Christopher Columbus recorded the occasion of his landing on Cuban soil for the first time, on 28 October 1492: 'Along the banks of the river were trees I have never seen at home, with flowers and fruit of the most diverse kinds, among the branches of which one heard the delightful chirping of birds... When I descended from the launch, I approached two fishermen's huts. Upon seeing me, the natives took fright and fled... This island is truly the most beautiful land human eyes have ever beheld.'

There are two sections to the resort. The first is older, with a village feel to it, and is centred around Playa Guardalavaca. The crescent-shaped beach itself is 4km (2½ miles) long, enclosed at both ends by rocks, and backed by abundant vegetation. The second is a few kilometres west, around Playa Esmeralda. The newer, mostly all-inclusive resort hotels are here, with excellent facilities, although there is not much to do outside the hotel complex. Nevertheless, the beach (also known as Estero Ciego) is perfect for snorkelling.

Bahía de Naranjo

West of the beach is a natural park called Bahía de Naranjo, which is well known for its marina and aquarium. Sailing trips and sailing expeditions can be arranged from here, while the dolphin and sea lion shows at the aquarium are often included in tours of the area.

Chorro de Maita

For those interested in archaeology, this site is unmissable. It is the largest native Indian necropolis in Cuba and the Caribbean, where 56 Taíno skeletons dating from 1490–1540 are preserved just as they were found. Although the museum is small, it is very well presented. A reconstruction of a pre-Columbian rural village is also here, with life-size statues of the natives. *Cerro de Yaguajay, Banes. Open: daily 9am–5pm. Admission charge.*

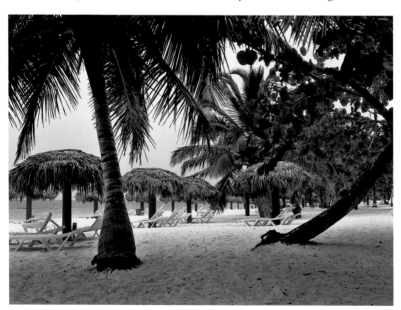

The beach at Guardalavaca

Eastern Central Cuba

The statue of General Calixto García in the Plaza Central, Holguín

HOLGUÍN

The town of Holguín is a good base to explore some of the more interesting sights in the province of the same name, such as Bahía de Bariay where Columbus landed, and some of the best beaches in Cuba, particularly in Guardalavaca.

The town itself is attractive and modern, with many leafy squares, hence its description as the 'city of parks'. Holguín was founded in 1545, and is named after García Holguín, a Spanish captain who helped colonise the area. Most of the architecture dates from the 19th and 20th centuries, and the streets have an air of pleasant tranquillity. It may have to do with the slow pace of the traffic, which is cluttered by hundreds of bicycles, the preferred form of transport for most residents.

The heart of the town is centred around Parque García (known commonly as Parque Central), with two parallel streets, Maceo and Libertad, forming the borders that contain the three main squares in the town: Parque Central, Parque Infantil and Parque Céspedes.

Plaza Central (Parque Calixto García)

Many of the sights of interest in this town are around this square, including the Museo Provincial. It was named after General Calixto García Iñiguez, who captured the town from the Spanish in 1872 during the Wars of Independence, and his statue stands in the middle of the square. One block from the plaza is the building where he was born, **Casa Natal de Calixto García**. The square really comes to life at night when families and friends congregate to enjoy the cool air, and listen to the music coming from nearby bars, especially the excellent Casa de la Trova.

Loma de la Cruz

Called 'Hill of the Cross', there are marvellous views from the top, a feature that was utilised by the town engineers. A cross was placed here on 3 May 1790 by a Franciscan priest, but it was blown down in 1998 by Hurricane Georges. Every 3 May, locals commemorate the occasion, called

Romerías de la Cruz de Mayo.
There is also a lookout tower built
by the Spanish, 127m (417ft) above
the town.
*The hill is 3km (2 miles) northwest of
Parque Calixto García and may be
ascended on foot (there are about 450
steps) or by road.*

Museo de Historia Natural

This is one of the most interesting
natural history museums in Cuba,
with an impressive collection of birds
and shells. There are 11 rooms with
7,000 specimens, including a 60-
million-year-old fossilised fish. The
museum contains many stuffed
animals, including a manatee and a
giant turtle, and the building is also
attractive, with neoclassical pillars and
Moorish turrets.
*Calle Maceo 129, between Martí and Luz
Caballero. Just off Parque Calixto García.*

*Open: Tue–Sat 9am–10pm, Sun
9am–9pm. Admission charge.*

Museo Provincial ('La Periquera')

The name 'parrot cage' for this museum
comes from the brightly coloured
soldiers who guarded the barracks in the
19th century, who came to be known as
periquitos (parakeets). The museum
illustrates the history of Holguín,
including its important role in the wars
of independence, which liberated the
city from the Spanish in 1872. Also
exhibited are archaeological relics of the
Taíno Indians from the 8th to the 15th
centuries. The most famous item is a
carved stone axe head, the *Hacha de
Holguín*, now the symbol of the city.
*Calle Frexes 198, between Manduley and
Maceo. Overlooks Parque Calixto García.
Tel: 463395. Open: Mon–Fri 8am–9pm,
Sat & Sun 9am–5pm. Admission charge,
plus charge for taking photos.*

View of the city from the steps of La Loma de la Cruz

Santiago de Cuba

Santiago de Cuba is a wholly different proposition to Havana or indeed to any other Cuban city. Its position at the eastern end of the island has given it a very Caribbean flavour in terms of climate, people and culture. As the second city in Cuba after Havana, it is of great importance to the traveller in understanding the country, its culture and history.

The city is protected from sea breezes, and sits in a bay surrounded by mountains, making it several degrees warmer than Havana. It is more musical, more passionate and livelier than the rest of the island, and is most famous for its Carnival each July, an experience full of colour, energy and

Santiago de Cuba town centre

raucous celebration. Some travellers notice the more brazen nature of locals approaching foreigners in the street, offering accommodation, a meal, or transport among other things. Do not come expecting beautiful colonial architecture, wide avenues and tranquil streets. However, the residents are friendly, lively and love to dance the night away. Once you get used to the rhythm of the city and the nature of the locals, you will enjoy Santiago de Cuba.

Indomitable character

The city is known as the 'Cradle of the Revolution'. It was in Santiago that Fidel Castro launched the struggle against dictator Batista by attacking the Moncada barracks in 1953, and it was in the nearby mountains of the Sierra Maestra that Castro and Che Guevara planned the guerrilla warfare that was to lead to the triumph of the Cuban Revolution. One hundred years earlier, local nationalists led the wars of independence against the Spanish.

The city is one of the oldest in the country, with many sites of historical and cultural interest, as well as many excursions to take you away from the traffic and fumes of the city, with visits to lovely beaches and scenic landscapes.

Architecture and culture

The city centre itself feels cluttered, with more energy and noise than other Cuban towns, but with buildings in

A view of Santiago Bay

much better condition than in Havana. It certainly does not have the colonial beauty of Trinidad, but it has an eclectic mix of architectural styles and colour.

The people and music have a distinctly Afro-Caribbean emphasis, with the religion *santería* playing an important role in many people's lives. The music is influenced by the large numbers of immigrants that came here from French colonies, particularly Haiti, and the music and dancing are certainly more energetic, especially noticeable at carnival time.

AROUND PARQUE CÉSPEDES

Parque Céspedes is the heart of the town, with many of the sights and museums within easy walking distance. Formerly the Plaza de Armas, it was renamed Parque Céspedes in honour of the nation's founding father, whose statue stands in the middle. It is very well maintained and policed, in an attempt to make the square as attractive to tourists as possible. Neoclassical in style, the square is flanked on the east side by the luxurious Hotel Casa Granda. Calle Heredia, which runs along one side of the square, is the most famous and lively street in the town, especially at night, when music venues such as the Casa de la Trova kick into action.

Parque Céspedes flanked by Hotel Casa Granda and the Cathedral

A colourful mural on Calle Heredia

Casa Natal de José María Heredia

This is a more modest house than that of Diego Velázquez (*see p118*), but it has an understated elegance. A national monument, it is the birthplace of the famous Cuban poet José María Heredia, who is credited with transforming Latin American poetry. He was exiled at the age of 20 for his involvement in an independence conspiracy and wrote his most famous ode to nature, *Niagara*, in the USA before his tragic death at the age of 36. This 18th-century house is very well preserved, and contains period wooden ceilings, tiled floors and furniture. The courtyard is pretty, with wooden columns, vegetation and a stone well. The building is also used as a cultural centre, with weekly poetry workshops. *Heredia 260, between Hartmann and Pío*

Rosado (Carnicería). Tel: 625350. Open: Tue–Sat 9am–7pm, Sun 9am–2pm. Admission charge.

Catedral de Nuestra Señora de la Asunción

The cathedral of Santiago has had a troubled history, needing to be rebuilt four times on account of a combination of earthquakes, pirate attacks and other disasters. This national monument stands out among the beautiful buildings around Parque Céspedes, and its most recent restoration has been a great success. The original building dates from 1524, with the most recent changes being made in 1922. As a result, there are a number of styles on display.
Calle Heredia, on the south side of Parque Céspedes. Tel: 628502. Open:

Tue–Fri 8am–noon & 5–6.30pm, Sat 8am–noon & 4–5pm. Services Tue–Fri 6.30pm, Sat 5pm, Sun 9am & 6.30pm.

Hotel Casa Granda

There are many points of interest at this hotel, which is one of the most elegant buildings in Santiago. Opened in 1914, it was patronised by many stars of the time, including Babe Ruth and Joe Louis. Graham Greene described it in his famous novel *Our Man in Havana* as a hotel frequented by spies. Now it is the perfect place to have a drink or snack at the terrace bar and café, and watch the activity in Parque Céspedes, or to enjoy the views over the city from the fifth floor. It is also a useful place for internet access, while the offices under the hotel offer tourist and exchange services (the Asistur office is the only place in Cuba that accepts American Express traveller's cheques).

Heredia 201, on the east side of Parque Céspedes. Tel: 686600. Charge for going up to the fifth floor bar 8pm–1am, but this buys you your first cocktail.

Museo de Ambiente Cubano

Perhaps the best museum in the town, and certainly the one with most character, is the Museo de Ambiente Cubano. It is the oldest private home in Cuba, and is full of furniture, china, porcelain and other objects. One really gets a feel for how the residents lived at the time. It was built around 1530 as a residence for Governor Diego Velázquez, who conquered Cuba. He lived on the top floor, while the ground floor, which was used to smelt gold, was called the 'House of Transactions'. One can still see the old furnace where the gold ingots were made. Each room shows a particular period of history, including Creole furniture from the 16th century, 19th-century furniture heavily influenced by the French style, and 19th-century stained-glass windows. A guided tour is recommended.

Calle Félix Pena 612, on the northwest corner of Parque Céspedes. Tel: 652652. Open: Mon–Sat 9am–5pm, Sun 9am–noon. Admission charge, plus charges for tours and taking photos.

Museo El Carnaval

If you are not able to attend the Santiago Carnival in July, this is the next best

---

SANTIAGO'S CARNIVAL

Carnival in Santiago is based on many African and Franco-Haitian elements, most of them religious. Festivities have been held between 24 June and 26 July in Santiago since the end of the 17th century, with the aim of honouring the city's patron saint, Santiago Apóstol (Saint James the Apostle). In the 17th century, slaves were allowed into the streets after the processions to sing, dance and play music. These were the forerunners of the Carnival groups, or *comparsas*, who wear masks or costumes, and carry streamers and banners and brightly coloured paper lamps (*farolas*). The chief dance is the *conga*, where people form a procession and dance through the streets. The whole town erupts into a frenzy of celebration and partying during the second half of July, a truly memorable experience.

The dining room in the Museo de Ambiente Cubano

thing. Among the exhibits are musical instruments, papier-mâché masks, banners and costumes, all of which give a flavour of this most famous of festivities. The courtyard of this lovely 18th-century building is used for folk events and concerts, as well as rehearsals by performers at the Carnival.

Calle Heredia 303, corner of Pío Rosado (Carnicería). Tel: 626955.
Open: Mon 3–5pm, Tue–Sat 9am–5.15pm, Sun 9am–noon. Admission charge.

Museo Emilio Bacardí Moreau

The oldest and perhaps the most eclectic museum in Cuba houses mementoes of the Wars of Independence, mummies from Egypt and South America, and both colonial and modern Cuban paintings. A tour is recommended.

The museum was named after the main benefactor, the industrialist and founder of the famous rum distillery, Emilio Bacardí Moreau. He was the first mayor of Cuba when it became a republic. The museum was founded in 1828, and the building was purpose-built in the neoclassical style.

Calle Pío Rosado, corner of Aguilera, two blocks east of the Parque Central. Tel: 628402. Open: Mon 1–4.30pm, Tue–Sat 8am–4pm. Admission charge.

Walk: Parque Céspedes, Santiago de Cuba

This area in the centre of Santiago is the most pleasant in the town, with well-restored buildings and lots of sights of historical and cultural interest.

Allow 4 hours.

The walk starts in Parque Céspedes. The streets in this area are often busy, with vehicles of every description as well as people. Locals may try to offer you some kind of service, and it is best to be easy-going but firm. Remember not to rush around, as the heat can be exhausting.

1 Museo de Ambiente Cubano

The home of the Spanish conquistador Diego Velázquez has been lovingly preserved, and is one of the most fascinating museums in Cuba. Remember to get a guide, as there is little written explanation of the exhibits.
Turn left on Félix Pena and right on Aguilera.

2 Ayuntamiento (Casa del Gobierno)

Although this white Moorish building is not open to the public, it is historically important. It was here that Fidel Castro made his first speech to the Cuban people on 1 January 1959, the day that dictator Batista fled the country and the Cuban Revolution triumphed. This building was built in 1950 to 18th-century designs and is now used as the town hall.
Facing the square, turn left and walk eastwards along Aguilera for two blocks, until you reach a white neoclassical building on your right.

3 Museo Emilio Bacardí Moreau

This houses an eclectic range of exhibits, including historical artefacts, colonial paintings, modern art and archaeology. A guided tour is recommended in order to make the most of the museum.
Walking down the steps of the museum, turn right then right onto Calle Heredia, perhaps the most famous street in the town, looking at the buildings on your left.

4 Casa Natal de José María Heredia

This modest but elegant museum was the birthplace of the famous Cuban poet José María Heredia, with some beautiful furniture and antique lamps. The shaded courtyard will give you a welcome break from the heat.

Continue walking west along Calle Heredia, crossing Hartmann and looking up to the left.

5 Casa de la Trova

This famous music venue is one of the most popular in town for live Cuban music. More touristy than other music venues, it still retains its vibrancy and character, especially at night.

Looking towards Parque Céspedes, cross Lacret.

6 Catedral de Nuestra Señora de la Asunción

The cathedral of Santiago is very well preserved, although it has been rebuilt

several times. The façade is neoclassical while the original church was built four centuries ago. Some say that Diego Velázquez is buried beneath the building.

Continue walking westwards along Heredia and turn left when you reach Corona. Look right when you reach the corner of this block.

7 Balcón de Velázquez

This spacious terrace offers a grand view of the port and bay of Santiago, as well as the picturesque quarter of Tivolí. It was built on the site of a Spanish fortress. There is an admission charge here, but the views are well worth it. You can also buy drinks and sit in the shade to recover from the exertions of the walk.

Walk: Parque Céspedes, Santiago de Cuba

BEYOND THE CITY CENTRE

Venturing out of the heart of the city is recommended, as Santiago de Cuba has several interesting sites of historical importance, particularly the Moncada Barracks. Some are only a short walk from Parque Céspedes, such as the Padre Pico steps and the Museo de la Lucha Clandestina.

Calle Saco

This important street (also called 'Enramada') links the old city with the port and is Santiago's main commercial street. The area nearest Parque Céspedes is a working-class quarter with some interesting early 20th-century wooden houses. At the bottom of the sloping street is the Paseo Marítimo, which retains the original paving from the 1840s, although it has lost its former elegance as the seafront promenade for the colonial city's high society. The promenade stretches out along the port.

Casa Natal de Antonio Maceo Grajales

One of the great generals in the Wars of Independence was born in this modest house in 1845. Maceo rejected the peace agreement in 1878 that ended the Ten Years War against the Spanish, and, after a period in exile, returned to liberate the island in the final and decisive War of Independence by 1898. The museum houses his personal belongings, including family photographs.

207 Los Maceo, between Calles Corona and Rastro. Tel: 623750. Open: Mon–Sat 9am–5pm. Admission charge.

Cementerio de Santa Ifigenia

This is a grand and well-kept cemetery which is the second most important on the island after the Colón cemetery in Havana. It contains graves, tombs and monuments of some of Cuba's patriotic heroes, most notable of which is José Martí's mausoleum. This large octagonal structure is surrounded by six statues of women, representing the six Cuban

THE ATTACK ON THE MONCADA BARRACKS

The attack on the Moncada Barracks on 26 July 1953 marked a turning point in the revolutionary struggle from peaceful means to armed conflict. The aim of the attack was to capture the barracks with its huge arsenal of weapons, and take control of the neighbourhood, which included a hospital and law courts. Using popular support in the area, they hoped that their revolution would quickly spread beyond the city. With a force of 100-odd rebels, Castro used the noisy carnival celebrations as the perfect time to launch the daring raid. The attack failed mainly because they ran into an army patrol, and the ensuing gunfight raised the 800-strong garrison from their sleep. Hopelessly outnumbered, eight of the rebels were killed and 55 were taken prisoner, tortured and executed. Fidel Castro and many others were captured in the nearby mountains but their lives were saved by the capturing army officer who recognised Castro from his university days. Castro was to resume the revolutionary struggle after his period in prison and exile when he landed in Cuba in December 1956 on the yacht *Granma*.

provinces in the 19th century. The statue of Martí inside is designed to receive a shaft of light all morning. Other tombs include those of the independence fighters Carlos Manuel de Céspedes, Emilio Bacardí (of the rum family) and Tomás Estrada Palma, who was the first president of Cuba. It is said that Fidel Castro will be buried here.

Avenida Crombet, Reparto Juan G Gómez, in the northwest of the city. Tel: 632723. Open: daily 7am–6pm. Admission charge, plus charge for taking photos. Includes guided tour.

Cuartel Moncada (Museo 26 de Julio)

One of the most important events in Cuba's history happened here in the Moncada Barracks, now a school and home to the Museo 26 de Julio. This was the site of the failed attack by Fidel Castro's revolutionaries on the second largest garrison in Cuba on 26 July 1953. This led to the capture and execution of many of the revolutionaries, and the imprisonment and exile of others, including Fidel Castro.

The bullet holes from the attack have been left on the building walls, while there is a detailed and fascinating exhibition on the events of the day, as well as the Cuban revolutionary struggle of the late 1950s. It includes blood-stained uniforms from that fateful day and possessions used by the revolutionaries in their struggle. A guided tour is recommended as the exhibits are explained in Spanish.

The Moncada Barracks, marked by bullet holes from the 1953 attack

Calle General Portuondo (Trinidad), between Moncada and Avenida de los Libertadores. Tel: 620157. Open: Tue–Sat 9.30am–5.15pm, Sun 9.15am–12.30pm. Admission charge, plus charge for taking photos.

Museo Abel Santamaría

For those interested in the Cuban Revolution, this museum is also worth visiting. It is part of the Parque Histórico Abel Santamaría, which also includes the Moncada Barracks, Saturnino Lora hospital and the law court buildings.

In the 1953 raid on the Moncada Barracks, a group of men led by Abel Santamaría targeted the Saturnino hospital, a strategic site on a hill overlooking the barracks. They were captured, tortured and killed, with Santamaría having his eyes gouged out.

Now all Cuban eye hospitals bear his name.

This museum focuses primarily on the trial of Fidel Castro and his men, held a few days after the attack. Castro's landmark self-defence speech manuscript is housed here, the now legendary 'History Will Absolve Me' speech. There are also photos showing the great hardship, socially and economically, that Cuba underwent during the 1950s.

Calle General Portuondo, corner of Avenida de los Libertadores. Tel: 624119. Open: Mon–Sat 9am–5pm. Admission charge.

Museo de la Lucha Clandestina

One of the most beautiful colonial buildings in the city (Loma del

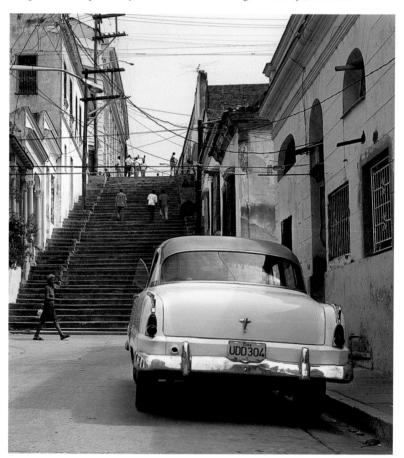

The famous Padre Pico steps leading to the Tivolí area

Intendente), this yellow building houses the Museum of the Clandestine Struggle, giving an interesting account of the activities of the Movimiento 26 de Julio, the underground struggle against Batista's dictatorship. The building, which was originally the headquarters of Batista's police, was a prime target for the revolutionaries, and was burnt down in 1956. The exhibits revolve around Frank País, the leader of the movement, who led a revolt in Santiago that tried to coincide with the landing of Fidel Castro's revolutionaries in Cuba in December 1956. The revolt was repressed and País was assassinated by Batista's police the following year.

Frank País's funeral was massively attended by local people, a signal that the Revolution would have significant local support. Other photos document the years of tension and conflict which led up to the rebels' triumph.

Calle Jesús Rabí 1, between Santa Rita and San Carlos, at the top of the Padre Pico steps. Tel: 624689. Open: Tue–Sun 9am–5pm. Admission charge, which includes an English-speaking guide. Exhibits are in Spanish.

Padre Pico steps

These steps leading up to the Tivolí area of the city are famous partly because the opening shots in Fidel Castro's first offensive against Batista were fired from here. The steps were named after Bernardo del Pico, a priest who helped the poor in Santiago, and built by Emilio Bacardí, the mayor at the time and founder of the famous rum factory. The steps lead to the most colourful neighbourhood in the city, populated in the late 1700s by newly arrived French immigrants who were escaping the revolution in Haiti. The Tivolí area was named after the theatre built there.

One of the most original and best music venues in the city is in this area, the **Casa de las Tradiciones** on Jesús Rabí, a few blocks south from the Museo de la Lucha Clandestina. Today the steps are home to domino and chess players, who sit all day enjoying a quiet game.

Near the bottom of Castillo Duany. The steps lead up to the Museo de la Lucha Clandestina and Calle Padre Pico.

Plaza de la Revolución

This rather soulless square is dominated by a huge and impressive monument, showing General Antonio Maceo, the 19th-century revolutionary, on horseback, surrounded by stylised representations of machetes. The monument is distinctly Soviet in style, being constructed in the early 1990s by Alberto Lezcay, a local sculptor.

It is in this square that major speeches and rallies are held, including the Mass said by Pope John Paul II during his visit in 1998.

In the block where Avenida de las Américas meets Avenida de los Libertadores (Carretera Central).

EXCURSIONS FROM SANTIAGO DE CUBA

A wide range of excursions is possible from Santiago. Some are available as day trips using one of the many tour agencies, while for some you may need to organise your own transport. The Rumbos office opposite Hotel Casa Granda is perhaps the most used, although you can also book tours at many of the big hotels outside the city centre. Overall, they are excellent value, enabling you to visit several sights in one day, often with lunch included.

Castillo del Morro San Pedro de la Roca

A hugely interesting and picturesque sight is the historic Castillo del Morro, an imposing cliff-top fort at the entrance to the bay of Santiago. It has been declared a UNESCO World Heritage Site, and has been relatively well maintained, even though it is nearly 370 years old. It was built by Giovan Battista Antonelli upon the order of the governor of the time, as a much-needed defence against pirates and corsairs (mercenary ships commissioned by enemy countries). There are many rooms worth visiting, including the munitions room, prison cells, chapel, and torture rooms. The bay was the scene of the decisive naval battle in which the US fleet attacked the city and defeated the Spanish fleet, which led to the independence of Cuba. Every evening at sunset, there is a ceremonial firing of a cannon.

The impressive Castillo del Morro stands sentinel over Cuba's southeast coast

Carretera del Morro, 10km (6 miles) southwest of Santiago. Tel: 691569. Open: daily 8am–8pm. Admission charge, plus charge for taking photos.

Cayo Granma

Often included in tours to the Castillo del Morro, this is home to a picturesque little fishing island, made up of multicoloured huts and small houses, some of which are on stilts in the water. It only takes about 30 minutes to walk around the island, and is a good way to see the locals' way of life in a relaxing environment. There are no vehicles, which makes it an enjoyable place to stroll. Cayo Granma was originally named Cayo Smith, after its wealthy owner, and it was at one time a resort for the rich.

Cayo Granma can be accessed by ferry from Marina Punta, 8km (5 miles) southwest of Santiago, at the end of Carretera Turística.

'El Cobre'

An attractive church in a picture-book setting, El Sanctuario de Nuestra Señora de la Caridad del Cobre (El Cobre) is the most famous church in Cuba. It contains the shrine of Cuba's patron saint, the Virgen de la Caridad del Cobre, a wooden statue of a black Madonna.

There are pilgrimages to the church from all over the country, and many mementoes are donated in gratitude, some of which are displayed. They include Ernest Hemingway's Nobel Prize medal, cups and medals from Cuban sports heroes, and earth collected by Cuban soldiers who fought in Angola. The statue of the Virgin is richly dressed with gold and jewels, and kept in an air-conditioned box, which revolves to face the basilica for Mass. Nearby is a copper (*cobre*) mine, which was worked by hundreds of slaves until 1807.

Village of El Cobre, 16km (10 miles) west of Santiago, off Carretera Central 21. Open: daily 8am–6pm. There is an annual procession here on 8 September. Women with exposed shoulders are not admitted, although coveralls can be hired

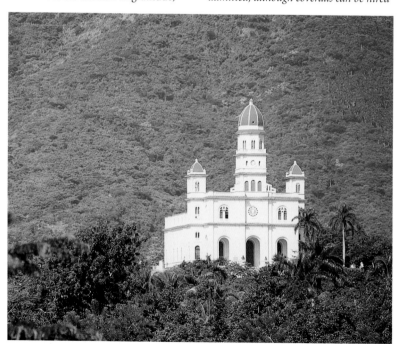

The church of El Cobre

if necessary. There are many touts selling flowers and candles for offering at the church, as well as youths pestering you to buy bits of copper rock for a few cents.

Gran Piedra

This is one of the area's most popular excursions, the main draw being the spectacular view from the top of this giant rock, which rests on the crater of an extinct volcano. Well over 1,000m (3,280ft) tall, and weighing 75,000 tonnes (73,820 tons), it can be reached by climbing the 450-odd steps from the road. The drive here takes you around hairpin bends and into cooler temperatures as you ascend. It is worth the journey, as the view of the lush countryside is one of the best in Cuba. Some say that one can see Haiti and Jamaica on a clear day, and their lights at night.

LA VIRGEN DEL COBRE

Legend has it that in 1606 three fishermen in the Bay of Nipe were about to capsize when they found the statue of the Virgin nailed to a plank of wood, floating in the sea. They were saved and brought the statue to the church, where it soon became an object of veneration for locals, even non-Catholics, who attributed miraculous powers to it. The mixture of African cult beliefs brought by the slaves and Spanish Roman Catholicism has developed a range of corresponding saints and gods. For example, the Virgin is associated with the Afro-Cuban goddess Ochún, who is always depicted as a beautiful black woman wearing yellow.

Jardín Botánico, 26km (16 miles) east of Santiago. Open: daily. Admission charge.

La Granjita Siboney

Another important historical site linked to the Cuban Revolution is this farmhouse, used as the headquarters

The ramparts of Castillo del Morro

and base in the run-up to the assault on the Moncada Barracks. It is now a museum containing uniforms, weapons and artefacts, as well as newspaper accounts of the attacks. It was rented in 1953 by Abel Santamaría, the only revolutionary originally from Santiago. It is said that many of the bodies of the executed revolutionaries from the attack on the barracks were taken here and guns placed by their bodies to make it look as though Batista's men had killed them in a gun battle at the farmhouse.

Carretera de la Gran Piedra, 16km (10 miles) east of Santiago. Open: daily 9am–5pm daily. Admission charge.

Museo Isabelica

One of numerous old coffee plantations around the Gran Piedra, but the best maintained, is this museum, once the home of French landowners from Haiti. It is a fascinating museum which gives an authentic impression of life on a 19th-century coffee plantation. The downstairs was used by labourers and for the storage of tools, while the upstairs was the living quarters of the owners. The plantation was named after Isabel María, the lover and house-slave of the owner, Victor Constantin. When slavery was abolished, he fled and – according to legend, at least – Isabel was thrown by the former slaves into a burning oven.

Carretera de la Gran Piedra 14km (9 miles) east of Santiago. It is within walking distance of Gran Piedra via a path from the foot of the rock. Open: daily 8am–4pm. Admission charge.

Valle de la Prehistoria

One of the most original amusement parks in the country is this huge children's park which includes a Natural History Museum. It is divided into areas according to evolutionary periods and features life-size models of dinosaurs and Stone Age men. It is well worth engaging an English-speaking guide who will give fascinating information on the prehistoric animals and an explanation of their evolution. Remember to take a hat and lots of water, as it can get very hot walking around in the scorching sun, and there is little shade.

Carretera Baconao 6.5km. Tel: 639239. Open: daily 8am–4.45pm. Admission charge.

THE ORIGINS OF COFFEE GROWING IN CUBA

French coffee growers in Haiti were forced to flee that country in 1791 on account of the revolution there, and the nearest island was Cuba. By this time, coffee was already a popular drink among the European bourgeoisie. Soon, the hills around Santiago and the area between Guantánamo and Baracoa were full of coffee trees. The land here was ideal as it offered both shade and water, and the demand for coffee was such that by 1820 there were 191 plantations, and around 42,000 imported slaves. French growers made their fortunes and built impressive manor houses on their plantations.

Tour: Eastern environs of Santiago

The east of Santiago is full of places to visit, from historical sights and children's attractions, to places in which to enjoy nature at its best. The area is known as Parque Baconao, and has been declared a biosphere reserve by UNESCO, having been developed mainly in the 1980s.

Allow a whole day.

The tour starts in Santiago de Cuba and takes you along the main sights east of the city. You can choose to stop the tour at Valle de la Prehistoria, or continue on for another 25km (16 miles) or so to the final sight on the tour, the aquarium. The road going east out of the city is the Carretera Siboney which takes you along the coast.

The road passes Abel Santamaría and Sevilla and divides at a village called Las Guásimas. Take the left-hand road, signposted to Gran Piedra. This steep road winds its way for 12km (7½ miles) up the hillside. Tour buses often stop for passengers to admire the coffee trees by the roadside and souvenir stalls.

1 Gran Piedra

This enormous monolith is at an altitude of 1,230m (4,035ft), with spectacular views of the surrounding tropical and mountain forests. You may not be able to see Haiti and Jamaica, but the view is certainly worth climbing the 450-odd steps from the bottom.

Drive back down for 2km (1 mile), until you reach 'Jardines de la Siberia'. Turn left.

2 Cafetal Isabelica

This is one of the few former coffee plantations in the area not in ruins, and it was once owned by French émigrés from Haiti. The buildings now house a museum, and you can see a demonstration of how coffee is grown and processed.

Continue down the road towards Las Guásimas, and turn left there to get back onto the Carretera Siboney. Drive for a couple of kilometres, looking out for a white and red farmhouse on the right.

3 La Granjita Siboney

This historical site is important because it was the base of operations for young revolutionaries in 1953, from which they launched their attack on the Moncada Barracks. The building is now a museum with uniforms and other memorabilia from the time. There are stone tributes on the side of the road around the area commemorating the spots where some of the revolutionaries were killed after the Moncada Barracks attacks.

Continue along the Carretera Siboney and take the right-hand road at La Estrella, going southwards to Siboney.

4 Playa Siboney

An ideal stop for lunch, this is the nearest beach to Santiago. There are some private *paladar* restaurants and food stalls here. The beach is pleasant, and with a reef just offshore it is good for snorkelling.

Drive back to La Estrella and turn right to get back on the main provincial road heading east (Carretera Baconao). You will pass El Oasis and Damajayabo.

5 Valle de la Prehistoria

This huge children's park is worth stopping at for an hour or two, as it offers a fascinating insight into the prehistoric world. Fans of the *Jurassic Park* films will find it especially interesting to see this collection of lifelike dinosaurs. Remember to take lots of water and a hat, as it can get very hot here in the middle of the day.

Continue 25km (16 miles) eastwards along the coast, past El Cupey and El Verraco, on the road to Baconao.

6 Acuario Baconao

The aquarium and dolphinarium here are popular with children and adults alike. There are three dolphin and sea-lion shows per day, as well as excellent displays of turtles, sharks and other species of fish, which can be seen at close range from a subterranean tunnel. Visitors can swim with the dolphins for an extra fee.

Tour: Eastern environs of Santiago

The rest of eastern Cuba

Many visitors to the east of Cuba do not venture further than Santiago de Cuba, which is a shame considering the wealth of attractions that the area has to offer. There are several distinct areas, each of which has its own identity, and the provinces here are Granma, Santiago de Cuba and Guantánamo.

The majestic Sierra Maestra mountains to the west are strongly associated with the guerrilla war in the 1950s. Fidel Castro and the other revolutionaries landed in the southwest corner of the island before establishing guerrilla bases in the mountains nearby. The south coast has some beautiful beaches, while the road between Manzanillo and Cabo Cruz has some of the wildest and most spectacular scenery in the country.

The eastern tip of Cuba

The area around Santiago de Cuba is clad in pine forests and coffee plantations, while the Sierra Maestra mountains dominate the area, reaching almost to the sea.

Even more mountainous is the east of the island and the province of Guantánamo. Visitors will know the area mainly for the US naval base here, but there are other more interesting sights in the province. The area has a more Caribbean and French feel to it, being influenced by immigrants from the former French colony of Haiti, which is only 80km (50 miles) from Cuba's most easterly point. The coastal town of Baracoa attracts more intrepid travellers, not only because of its beautiful location on the tropical coast, but also because of its distinctive atmosphere and nightlife.

BARACOA

Although it is relatively isolated from the main tourist trails, Baracoa is gaining in popularity, especially with visitors who are attracted by its laid-back atmosphere, friendly people and lovely beaches. The Cubans have a saying, 'Baracoa means nature', which rings true, but the real origin of the name is from an Amerindian language, meaning 'existence of the sea'.

The area is a UNESCO biosphere reserve, with ten rivers, including the widest river in Cuba, the Río Toa. Baracoa provides 80 per cent of the country's coconut palms, while there are many beautiful waterfalls and

Forest around the Sagua-Baracoa mountain range

120 different types of tree. It is also the wettest region in Cuba.

Although just a small town, Baracoa's size belies its importance, since it is the oldest city in Cuba; the site was discovered by Christopher Columbus in 1492. The architecture is certainly not colonial, but is instead a mixture of styles, with much French influence. Luxurious vegetation is everywhere, and seems to invade the town itself, some wooden buildings being virtually overcome by nature.

The town was founded in 1512 by Diego Velázquez and called Nuestra Señora de la Asunción de Baracoa. It was the capital of Cuba for three years, before Velázquez transferred his residence to Santiago. This marked the beginning of a long period of isolation for the town, which has enabled the residents to maintain traditions and to preserve the environment. Through the centuries the town has supported itself by cultivating cocoa, coconuts and bananas, and by fishing. The town's isolation decreased in the 1960s with the building of the viaduct, La Farola, which has created one of the most spectacular roads on the island.

Baracoa is small and compact, and there are not many sights of any major significance, but a very pleasant walk can be had in the streets of the town centre.

Castillo de Seboruco

The view from the terrace of this 18th-century fortress is the best in town, looking over the roofs to the bay. It sits on a hill above the town and is now the Hotel El Castillo.
Calle Calixto García. Tel: 5165.

Catedral de Nuestra Señora de la Asunción

This church is most famous as the home of the Cruz de la Parra, a wooden cross that is said to be the oldest symbol of Christianity in the New World. According to legend, Christopher Columbus brought the cross on his first voyage to America, placing it on 1 December 1492 on the spot where Baracoa was later founded. This modest church was built in 1512, burnt down by the French, and rebuilt in 1805.

Calle Maceo 152. Open: Tue–Fri 8am–noon & 2–5pm, Sat 8am–noon, Sun Mass at 9am.

El Malecón

The ideal time to stroll along the seafront is during the week when it is quieter, as the road houses the bustling food market on Saturday mornings, while the *noche baracoesa*, a lively folk festival, is held here on Saturday nights. *El Malecón runs across the whole of the north seafront of the town, between Fuerte Matachí in the east and Fuerte de la Punta on the western tip.*

Hotel La Rusa

Halfway along the Malecón is this historic hotel, named after its original owner, Magdalena Rovenskaya, of aristocratic background, who left Russia in 1917 and ended up in Baracoa, building this hotel. She was affectionately known in the area as 'Mima', and she supported the Revolution with funds, entertaining Castro and Che at her hotel during the revolutionary struggle. She was later immortalised in the book *The Consecration of Spring* by Alejo Carpentier. The hotel has interesting photos and relics in the foyer.
Máximo Gómez 13. Tel: 43011.

Museo Municipal (Fuerte Matachín)

An interesting overview of local history is given in this small museum, housed in a colonial fortress built as a defence

against pirates. The museum has an impressive natural history section, including *Polymita* snails which are famous in the town. Another highlight is the only armaments magazine of its type in Cuba, dating from 1739.
Calle José Martí y Malecón. Tel: 42122. Open: daily 8am–noon & 2–6pm. Admission charge.

Parque Central (Parque Independencia)

The bust of the Indian leader Hatuey is located within this square, overlooked by the cathedral. The area comes to life in the evenings when residents young and old congregate here, although in the daytime there are many snack stalls selling good sandwiches and drinks. The Casa de la Trova is close by.

Excursions from Baracoa

There are some notable trips from the town which are worth mentioning.
Playa Maguana is a lovely beach 22km (14 miles) from Baracoa, with white sand. The most spectacular of Baracoa's rivers is the **Río Yumurí**, 30km (18 miles) east of the town. You can take an organised trip here to visit a *cacao* farm and to fish. Another worthwhile trip is to the top of **El Yunque** to view the breathtaking scenery from 575m (1,886ft) above sea level.

The rest of eastern Cuba

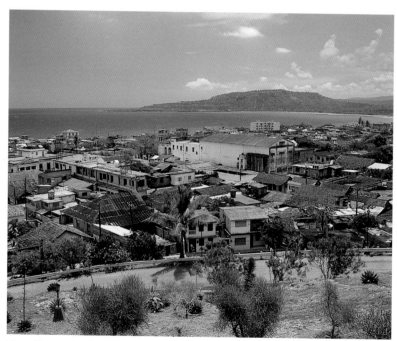

View of Baracoa Bay from Castillo de Seboruco

GUANTÁNAMO

It is said that if it were not for the US naval base here and the famous song 'Guantanamera', this town would only be known to Cubans and music fans. The town itself was founded in 1796 to take in the French fleeing from revolution in Haiti. This has influenced the architecture, which is much less Spanish in style than in many other Cuban cities. It has narrow, brightly coloured buildings and narrow balconies. The local music is also slightly different, with its origins in the coffee plantation culture of the 19th century.

The US naval base is not far from the town, but has no impact upon life in

Part of the US naval base at Guantánamo

the area. Visits can be made to the Mirador de Malones to view it through binoculars. Other than the naval base, there are few tourist sights in the town itself, although a walk around the well-restored town centre is pleasant.

Mirador de Malones

The US naval base is US territory in Cuba, granted by Cuba to the US Navy as part of the 1901 Platt Amendment. It covers 110sq km (40sq miles) and is surrounded by 27km (16 miles) of fence. The base is not open to the public but can be viewed from a purpose-built viewing point (*mirador*), used by the Cuban authorities to spy upon the base. Tours start in an underground museum where a Cuban military attaché explains the history of the naval base and the current political issues. You can then go up to the top of the hill, where

THE US NAVAL BASE

The American naval base at Guantánamo Bay was installed in 1903 as part of the Platt Amendment (1901), which was added to the new Cuban constitution by US Congress. This effectively made Cuba a protectorate of the USA, and gave the USA the right to have a naval base here. The Platt Amendment was repealed in 1934, but the lease on the base does not expire until 2033.

The existence of US territory on Cuban soil has fuelled much resentment against the USA even to this day. The $2,000 occupancy fee that the USA pays Cuba per year has been regularly returned to the USA since the Revolution. The base is effectively a remnant of the Cold War, with no military or political purpose other than a purely symbolic one. In the meantime, the USA spends many millions of dollars a year maintaining the base. In recent years, the USA has established detention centres on the base, housing several hundred terrorist suspects.

MUSIC IN GUANTÁNAMO

The full name of the famous song is 'Guajira Guantanamera', written about a proud local girl with a habit of ignoring compliments paid to her. Its composer, Joseito Fernández, wrote it in the 1940s, almost for fun. Later, verses from José Martí's *Versos Sencillos* were adapted to the music. This song is used by virtually all music groups in Cuba as the climax to the show, and remains as popular as ever.

One of the main music styles in the area is *changüí*, a variation of *son* music that developed in the coffee plantations in the mountains. It utilises old-style bongos and an African thumb bass, and is regarded as one of the most complex but beautiful forms of *son*. The *Tumba Francesa* is a colourful folk dance tradition, as well as the name of a well-known music venue in Guantánamo. The folk dance was created during the 1890s by newly freed black slaves to preserve the cultural heritage that had been developed in the plantations.

a telescope enables you to look at the base. Despite this being a military zone, you can film and take photographs.
24km (14¹/₂ miles) southeast of Guantánamo. The only way to view the base is by booking a tour at Villa Gaviota in Santiago or in Hotel Guantánamo in the town. You travel for 10km (6 miles) through forests of cacti in the military zone before reaching the viewing point.

Museo Provincial

This former prison now houses artefacts from the history of the province, including documents, photographs and memorabilia.
Plaza Martí, corner of Prado. Tel: 325872. Open: Tue–Sat 8am–noon & 2–6pm, Mon 2–6pm. Admission charge.

Museo Zoológico de Piedra

This unusual open-air museum was founded by Angel Iñigo, a farmer and self-taught sculptor. He has produced around 40 sculpted animals in stone,

from tiny stone lizards to huge bison, all carved directly from the rocks in a beautiful tropical setting.
Boquerón de Yateras. Open: daily 9am–6pm. Admission charge.

The original sheet music for 'Guajira Guantanamera'

Tour: From Manzanillo to Marea del Portillo

This is a fascinating area of the island, with dramatic coastal scenery where the Sierra Maestra mountains almost fall into the sea along the south coast. The landscape is wild at times, and unspoilt by tourist development. The area is also important historically, and there are several interesting sites to visit. Most important among these is the Parque Nacional Desembarco del Granma.

Allow at least a whole day for this driving tour. For a more relaxed drive, stay in Marea del Portillo, which is an excellent base for activities and excursions.

(See route on map, p138.)

The tour starts in Manzanillo, a small seaside town with little interest in developing tourism. In fact, there are few dollar facilities and almost everything is paid for in pesos. Take the provincial road No 4, heading southwest from Manzanillo, and drive 10km (6 miles) into the hills.

1 Parque Nacional La Demajagua

It was here in 1868 that Carlos Manuel de Céspedes effectively started the first War of Independence by liberating his slaves. The ruins of this sugar mill in the hills were named after the bell that was used to call slaves to work, which became the symbol of opposition to Spanish colonial rule. The estate still has sugar-making equipment, including *calderas* (vats) for making molasses. *From here, continue along the same road for 40km (25 miles).*

2 Media Luna

This small town was home to Celia Sánchez, a key figure at the beginning of the Revolution, who managed to get

The replica of the yacht *Granma*

The slopes of the Sierra Maestra

messages to different groups of revolutionaries when they were forced to scatter into the hills after the landing of *Granma* was met by Batista's troops. She later fought with Castro in the Sierra Maestra mountains and became his right-hand 'man' during the Revolution. She filled several important political positions after 1959 before dying of cancer in 1980. The house where she was born is now an interesting museum.

Continue for 23km (14 miles) along the same road (No 4), bearing right at the junction with provincial road No 20.

3 Niquero

The hotel in this village is a good place to stop for a drink or lunch. There are great views towards the sea, and of a sugar mill in the other direction, from the roof-top bar.

From Niquero, a dirt road takes you past Belic to Las Coloradas. An alternative stop for food or drinks is Campismo Las Coloradas, a restaurant and group of huts just 4km (2 miles) southwest of Belic.

4 Playa Las Coloradas

This is the historic heart of the Parque Nacional Desembarco del *Granma*. For it is in a mangrove swamp just southwest of Playa Las Coloradas that the yacht *Granma* landed with 82 of Fidel Castro's revolutionaries on 2 December 1956. By the road there is a small park where a replica of the *Granma* can be seen. A 2km (1-mile) concrete path through the

Tour from Manzanillo to Marea del Portillo

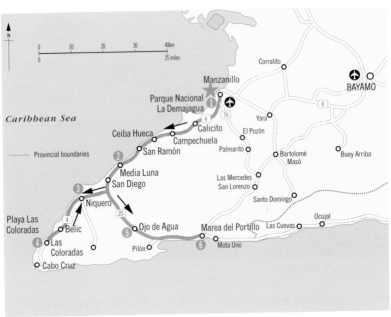

swamp takes you to the actual site, now a concrete jetty with a plaque. *Rather than continue along this road to Cabo Cruz, and the tip of the peninsula, turn back past Niquero and turn right at the junction with road No 20, heading southeast towards Pilón.*

5 Ojo de Agua

Before you reach Pilón you will see three separate signs and plaques marking the spots where the revolutionaries from the *Granma* crossed the road in underground water conduits, before heading into the Sierra Maestra. The signs have the emblems of five palms in a heart because the revolutionaries arranged to reassemble at a place called Cinco Palmas.

Once you pass Pilón, a sugar-producing town with a thriving commercial port, you continue east along the coastal road 15km (9 miles).

6 Marea del Portillo

This stretch of the south coast contains the best beaches in the area. The scenery too is superb, with palm-trees and bays of volcanic sand at the foot of the mountains.

There are a few hotels here, plus an inlet surrounded by rocks and a beach of black sand. Some are all-inclusive hotels, which are popular with Canadian package tours, but most offer good facilities for water sports, diving, boat trips, hikes and horse rides.

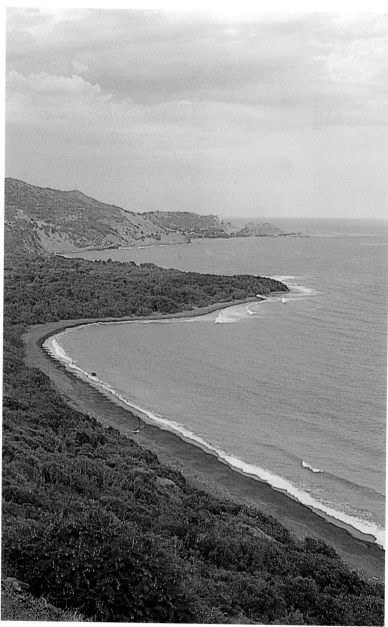

View of the spectacular southern coast

Getting away from it all

The island is blessed not only with national beauty in abundance, but also government policy that develops tourist facilities in a carefully managed way so as to minimise the impact on the environment. While Cuba is internationally famous for its diving and sailing, nature lovers will find the island a paradise for hiking, birdwatching and other ecotourist activities.

CYCLING

Cycling is increasingly popular, both as an activity to get away from the tourist centres, and as a means of seeing the island. It is a great way to enjoy the beautiful landscape and to get to know more of the real Cuba. Some travellers bring their bicycles to Cuba, while many tours and charity bike rides around the island, organised in the UK and elsewhere, take place during the cool season. Bicycles are available to rent from large hotels and holiday villages, and are generally of good quality, certainly much better than those used by the locals.

The country's infrastructure of roads is surprisingly extensive, and most of the country is accessible to cyclists. However, some of the roads are falling into disrepair, especially those in rural areas, and potholes are abundant. Traffic is generally light, particularly out of the main towns, and many Cubans have bicycles, because of the high cost of petrol.

If you are planning to cycle in Cuba, some preparation is essential. November to May is the best time of the year, when humidity is lower and tropical storms are infrequent. Cycling westwards is much easier, as there are strong year-round northeast winds. It is important to cycle only in the daytime, as roads are mainly unlit at night and can be dangerous.

In terms of where to go, there are many areas within striking distance of Havana, although the Sierra Maestra is a popular area with cycling tours. Cycling in Havana is a good way to see the city, although there is more traffic on the roads than before. Cruising the length of the Malecón is a must for foreign cyclists and locals alike, and there are some bicycle lanes and bicycle parking lots available. Outside the city, the Playas del Este can be reached on a day trip, while further from the city, Soroa, Las Terrazas and Viñales are accessible, although there are some steep climbs and sharp bends.

Further information can be obtained from *www.cyclecuba.net* and *sales@havanatour.co.uk*

DIVING AND SNORKELLING

Cuba is one of the best places in the Caribbean for diving, due to its huge coastline (5,700km or 3,500 miles) and number of small islands (over 4,000), and also because of the pristine nature of its marine environment. The government has been proactive in protecting marine life, with the result that Cuba does not suffer the problems of overharvesting and overdevelopment in dive sites that have beset its Caribbean neighbours.

Due to the coral reef and offshore islands (*cayos*), there are no strong currents and visibility is often more than 40m (131ft). There are now about 15 zones developed for diving, with updated accommodation on site, and virtually every beach resort now has at least one dive centre. Both wall and platform dives are available along the coral reef, while there are a number of fascinating shipwrecks to explore, on account of Cuba's history of piracy and colonial trade.

The main dive areas are as follows:
Isla de la Juventud, south of the mainland. Cuba's most famous dive area, a marine park, is being established around the island by the government. The main centre is El Colony, while there are other good centres at Cayo Largo, at the eastern end of the archipelago.

María La Gorda, in the far west of the island. Great diving in a warm, sheltered bay, with excellent visibility all year round.

Varadero, just east of Havana. One of the most developed areas for diving, with diving packages available. There are several sites around the offshore cays suitable for novice and advanced divers.

Archipiélago Jardines del Rey, on the north coast, north of Camagüey. There are two main dive areas in this large area. Santa Lucía has two dive shops and some fascinating historical wrecks, while Cayo Coco has beautifully clear water with large quantities of fish.

Santiago de Cuba area. There are two dive shops along the coast outside the

Varadero is one of the best places to go diving

The tocororo (Cuban trogon)

city: east of the city is **Sigua Dive Centre** (*Carretera Baconao, 28km*), while to the west is **Sierra Mar** (*Playa Sevilla, Guamá*).

There are also excellent dive sites in these other locations:

Faro de Luna, near Cienfuegos, has over 18 reef sites and a variety of modern wrecks.

Jardines de la Reina, 80km (50 miles) south of the province of Camagüey. These islands have been declared a natural park and divers need an expensive licence to dive.

Playa Girón, near the Bay of Pigs. There is a modern shipwreck here, intentionally sunk by the government for diving purposes.

Cayo Levisa, about 125km (78 miles) from Havana, on the northwest coast. The current is gentle, so this is an ideal spot for beginners.

Guardalavaca, along the northeast coast of the island in the province of Holguín. There are two dive shops at the resort hotels here. Lots of underwater life, but not recommended in the wet season.

HIKING

For hiking, the most developed areas are in the Viñales area, the Topes de Collantes area near Trinidad, and the Sierra Maestra National Park. There are regular tours from Trinidad around the Topes de Collantes, and you can take a refreshing dip in the natural pools here (cars will not take you all the way; 4 × 4 jeep tours are recommended).

In the Sierra Maestra, a popular trek is from Alto Naranjo to Las Cuevas. There is also a challenging 5km (3-mile) hike from Santo Domingo, the main base for the area, to the Alto Naranjo viewpoint (950m or 3,120ft high). Castro's forest HQ from the Revolution can be visited too, with a permit obtainable from the forest rangers, a lovely and sometimes difficult hour's walk through dense, often foggy forest.

Treks can be organised and guides hired in Villa Santo Domingo, and simple overnight accommodation is available. The facilities are spartan and some of the area is a military zone, not open to the public.

HORSE RIDING

Trekking on horseback is also popular, especially in the Viñales Valley. The only riding centre in Havana is in Parque Lenin, but in many ecotourist centres, resorts and camping areas, horse-riding facilities are available.

NATURE TOURISM

Nature lovers will find much to occupy them as Cuba is home to a vast array of flora and fauna, coupled with a responsible and proactive ecotourist policy from the government. The island contains 6,700 species of higher plants, half of which are endemic, as well as 14,000 invertebrate species and 650 vertebrate species, including 350 species of bird.

Natural highlights include the smallest frog in the world, only 12mm (¹/₂ inch) long, as well as the smallest bird in the world, the bee hummingbird (63mm/2¹/₂ inches). Cuba is home to 4 per cent of all the land species on the planet.

There are 116 nature trails to enjoy in Cuba, with a variety of landscapes. There are forests with unusual orchids, especially in western Cuba, dry mountainous areas with very old species of cactus, mangroves with tropical coastal ecosystems, wetlands with many biologically valuable species, and hummocks with rare fossil plants.

Ecotourist locations

Of particular interest to nature lovers is the Viñales Valley, declared part of the 'World Cultural Landscape' by UNESCO. It is internationally known for its beauty, the biodiversity of its vegetation and animal life, and it has the largest cave system in the West Indies.

The province of Pinar del Río also contains two biosphere reserves recognised by UNESCO: the Guanahacabibes peninsula in the far west of the island, and the Sierra del Rosario which includes Soroa,

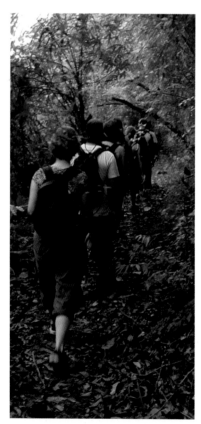

A trek through the forest at Las Terrazas

Las Terrazas and the Santo Tomás cave system.

The Sierra del Rosario and Viñales Valley are within easy striking distance of Havana, and there are many tours available, either as day excursions or as tours including an overnight stay (especially recommended if visiting the Viñales Valley). The Guanahacabibes peninsula can be reached by bus from Havana, with a change in Pinar del Río. Tours from Havana are popular, while there is more freedom of movement with a hired car.

Península de Zapata

The other main ecotourist area in Cuba is the Península de Zapata National Park and Biosphere Reserve which has a range of sites of interest: the Laguna del Tesoro, the Amerindian village of Guamá, La Boca crocodile breeding ground, and Playa Larga, to name the most important. This area is particularly suitable for birdwatchers, since the marshland ecosystem is a haven for hundreds of different species, including migratory birds. Among the 150 species of bird found in the Zapata Swamp, a UNESCO biosphere reserve, are the *zunzuncito*, the Cuban pygmy owl, a rare type of baldicoot called the Zapata rail, and waterhen. Manatees can be seen along the coast, while in the spring the beaches and roads are invaded by crabs leaving the water to mate.

The Península de Zapata can be visited by tours from Havana or Cienfuegos, and there are public buses on the Havana–Playa Girón route that stop in Playa Larga. However, a hired car is often more convenient in this area. It is well worth staying a few nights, especially for birdwatchers, who can be ready at dawn, before the tour buses arrive.

Further information

A number of travel agencies organise specialist tours for nature lovers, the main one being **Gaviota Tours**:
Gaviota Tours, Edificio La Marina, Avenida del Puerto 102 between Jústiz and Obrapía, Havana. Tel: 666777. www.gaviota-grupo.com.
For walking holidays in general, look at *www.ramblersholidays.co.uk* and *www.responsibletravel.com*

SAILING

The island is an ideal stopping-off point for yachts and sailing boats, and there are marinas offering moorings, boat rental and other services. The best time of the year for sailing is from December to April, when the weather is mild. However, the waters surrounding the island are generally calm, with plenty of bays.

The most popular area for sailing is the Archipiélago de los Canarreos, south of the mainland, and the biggest marina is the Marina Hemingway just west of Havana. The main marinas are owned by Cubanacán, Puertosol and Gaviota, which all offer a range of services, including excursions and boat hire.

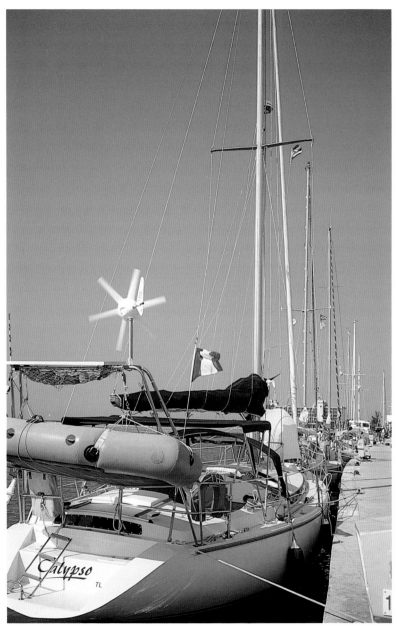

Sailing boats at the Marina Hemingway, Havana

Shopping

There are a growing number of shops in Cuba, and the choice of goods has improved considerably in recent years. The main places to buy these are at the tourist centres where quality is high. The main items bought by visitors to take home include cigars, rum and handicrafts.

State-run dollar shops, often situated in hotels, dominate the sale of souvenirs, but the legalisation of limited private enterprise has encouraged the growth of handicraft and food markets. These markets tend to have lower prices and bargaining is acceptable, compared to the higher-cost fixed-price state shops. Virtually all goods will need to be bought in CUC. Cuba is good value compared with the rest of the Caribbean, but more expensive than mainland Latin American countries.

Art

Art varies enormously in quality. One of the most popular styles is *naïf* paintings, inspired by the Afro-Caribbean culture and often depicting landscapes and views of colonial towns. The Feria del Tacón near the Castillo de Real Fuerza in Havana is an excellent place to see the work of talented young artists. Bear in mind that you need documentation to take works of art out of the country, but galleries and even market vendors can give you the necessary stamp and paperwork.

Black coral

The black coral from Cuban reefs is famous as a material for making jewellery. Importing black coral and/or tortoiseshell into your home country is illegal as both are protected. While items may look stunning, do the oceans and your criminal record a favour and leave them in the shops.

Books and CDs

It's worth buying books and CDs in Cuba. Remember that CDs of music that is popular in Cuba are unlikely to be found outside the country. So if you want to be certain of owning a CD from Cuban musicians such as Los Van Van and Silvio Rodríguez, it's best to buy them while you're in Cuba.

Cigars

Cuban cigars are the best in the world, and make an ideal luxury gift, especially when packed in elegant cedar boxes. Do not be tempted to buy cigars from people soliciting on the street, as these are likely to be low-quality fakes. Make sure that the box has a branded label *hecho in Cuba totalmente a mano* (totally hand-made in Cuba), the official government seal, and the *Habanos* band.

You can only take 50 cigars out of the country without a receipt, but if you buy them in a state shop and get a valid receipt you can buy cigars up to the value of US$2,000 (except if you are travelling to the USA, where the importation of Cuban cigars is prohibited).

For more information, see the feature on Cigars on pp78–9.

Handicrafts

There is a huge range of unusual handicrafts available for sale in Cuba, made from raw material such as bamboo, shells, seeds, banana leaves and other plant fibres.

An Afro-Caribbean painting in the *Naïf* style

Medicines

It may come as a surprise to many visitors that Cuba is one of the leading producers and exporters of pharmaceuticals. Some of the medicines available include PPG, an anti-cholesterol drug obtained from sugar cane which is also good for arteriosclerosis, and shark cartilage which strengthens bones and is especially good for children and older people. Food supplements include excellent honey, royal jelly and bee-glue (propolis), as well as spirulina which is derived from algae. International pharmacies and duty-free shops in the airport are good places to buy pharmaceuticals.

Musical instruments

Many traditional Cuban musical instruments can be bought in music stores and markets. These include bongos, maracas, claves and tumbadora drums, which are played with the hands. Also popular is the *güiro*, the gourd of the güira fruit, which is stroked with a small stick.

Papier mâché

This technique is a relatively recent introduction in Cuba but is generating many high-quality goods. Brightly coloured masks, models of vintage cars, and toys can be seen in many markets.

Perfumes

The government-owned Suchel Camacho company produces very good perfumes, as well as face and body creams, all at good prices. Brands include the spicy Coral Negro, and the flower-scented Mariposa.

Rum

The most famous brand in Cuba is 'Havana Club', whose distillery can be visited in Havana. There are many types of rum, with prices mostly based on their age and quality. The most common type is 'Silver Dry', a young clear rum, while others are aged for seven years or more, and are more highly prized. Do not be tempted to buy sugar cane spirit or cheap firewater, as these may make you ill. (*See pp50–51.*)

Wood

There is a large range of very well-made wooden sculptures and figures on sale in markets and state-run shops. Many are inspired by African traditions, often using cedar and rosewood. Carved cedarwood cigar boxes are always crafted elegantly. Wooden objects can also be found on sale in the Galerías del Arte.

WHERE TO SHOP

Havana

The capital has the best range of shops in the country, catering both for Cubans and tourists. However, shopping is not a leisure activity in Cuba, and the nearest you will get to this type of experience is at the big tourist hotels which have well-appointed, well-stocked shops. The shopping centres get very busy at weekends. The large department stores are mostly on Avenida de Italia (Galiano), between San Rafael and Neptuno.

Art: **Galería del Grabado** Original lithographs and other works of art can be purchased directly from the artists. *At the back of the Taller Experimental de Gráfica de La Habana, Callejón del Chorro 62, Plaza de la Catedral. Tel: 8620979.*

Books: **Instituto Cubano del Libro** has three bookshops. *Palacio del Segundo Cabo, O'Reilly 4 and Tacón. Tel: 8632244.*

Cigars: **Real Fábrica de Tabacos Partagás** This factory has a large shop selling a good range of cigars in lovely surroundings. *Industria, between Barcelona and Dragones (almost opposite the Capitolio).*

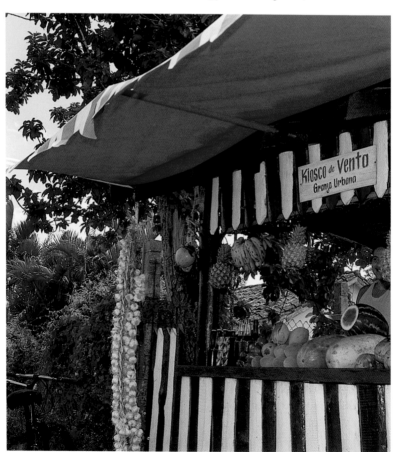

Roadside fruit stall, just outside Viñales

Food: **Harris Brothers** has the best selection in Old Havana. *Villegas, between San Juan de Dios and O'Reilly.*

Focsa Supermarket has a good range of food. *Calle 17, between Calles M and N, Vedado.*

Handicrafts: **Palacio de la Artesanía** A large selection of Cuban handicrafts, as well as other items not available elsewhere, such as footwear and clothing. *Palacio Pedroso, Cuba 64, between Peña Pobre and Cuarteles (opposite Parque Anfiteatro). Tel: 8671118.*

Music: **Artex** has a good selection of music. *Calle L, corner of Calle 23. Tel: 8383162.*

Open-air markets: **Feria del Tacón** is the city's largest craft market with a huge range of products. *Avenida Tacón, between Chacón and Empedrado, very near the Cathedral.* **Feria del 23** is a busy market with lots of home-made products. *Calle 23, opposite Pabellón Cuba, Vedado.*

Photography: **Publifoto** develops films, among other services. *Edificio Focsa, Calle M, between Calles 17 and 19, Vedado.* **Foto Habana**, *22 Tacón* sells a variety of camera-related articles.

Shopping centres: **Plaza de Carlos III** A wide range of shops including photography, cigars, sports and a supermarket. *Avenida Salvador Allende, between Arbol Seco and Retiro, Centro Habana.* **Galerías de Paseo** *Calle 1, between Paseo and A.* As well as a supermarket, clothes, shoes and homeware are sold.

Other items: **La Maison** has dollar shops selling cigars, handicrafts, jewellery and perfume. Also has fashion shows with imported clothes. *Calle 16 No 701 corner of Calle 7, Miramar.*

The **Caracol** chain of shops in tourist hotels (*one in the Habana Libre, Calle 23, Vedado*) sells tourist goods as well as luxury items such as chocolate, clothes, biscuits and wine.

Santiago de Cuba

There is a good range of shops in this city, many of which are around Parque Céspedes. Handicrafts and books are sold on the street on Heredia between Hartmann and Pío Rosado.

Artex Music and videos in the Casa de la Trova.

La Bombonera A dollar store selling food, very near Parque Céspedes. *Aguilera, between Lacret and Hartmann.*

Casa de la Artesanía A good range of hand-made products, including wooden carvings and some lovely furniture. *Under the cathedral in Parque Céspedes.*

Librería Internacional A good selection of books including paperbacks in English. *Heredia, under the cathedral.*

La Maison Expensive European clothes, dollars only. *Avenida Manduley.*

Photoservice Has several shops in town, *including one on General Lacret under the cathedral, another on Félix Pena between Aguilera and Enramada.*

Salón Artexanda Sells arts and crafts. *Heredia, between Calvario and Pío Rosado.*

Trinidad

There are not many shops in this small colonial town, although they do cater for tourists and offer a good selection of handicrafts.

Bazar Trinidad sells handicrafts, T-shirts, postcards and pictures. *Maceo 451, corner of Zerquera.*

Candonga (Mercado Popular de Artesanía). The whole street at Calle Toro is devoted to handicrafts, including contemporary art and handmade clothes.

Galería de Arte sells contemporary Cuban art. *Villena 43, opposite Plaza Mayor.*

Photoservice Photo services and goods. *José Martí, between Colón and Camilo Cienfuegos.*

Tienda Panamericana A dollar store selling clothes, food and toiletries. *Lino Pérez, between Cadahía and José Martí.*

Universo A department store. *Martí, between Zerquera and Colón.*

Hats for sale in Trinidad

Entertainment

There is a wealth of entertainment options in Cuba, mostly centring around music. Out of all the islands in the Caribbean, Cuba is renowned for having the best nightlife, and it is hard not to get caught up in the intoxicating rhythms and hip-swaying movements that permeate the many local music venues in every city.

Havana in particular has a range of options to suit all budgets. On many street corners, there will be music played and impromptu dancing, while in the tourist restaurants and bars groups of musicians come to play for a short while and gratefully receive any tips before moving on to the next location. Besides music, Cuba nurtures other forms of entertainment, from ballet and folk-dancing, to theatre, festivals and sporting activities.

At many Cuban airports a small guide called *Bienvenidos a Cuba* is available, which gives information on cultural events and shows, including addresses of venues. In Havana the free magazine *Cartelera* (*www.cartelera.com*) details upcoming events, while other towns have leaflets or posters pinned up in strategic locations to let you know what is happening and when. Hotels are also good sources of information, providing free leaflets and brochures.

Cinema

Cinema ticket prices are incredibly low, making it very popular with Cubans. Cuban cinema is called the 'seventh art' and the industry is thriving. There are almost 200 cinemas in Havana, showing both Cuban and international films.

Havana: **Yara** – one of the largest in the city, but often sold out at weekends. *Opposite Hotel Habana Libre. Tel: 8329430.* **Payret** – films shown continuously from 12.30pm. *Prado 503, corner of San José, Vedado. Tel: 8633163.*

Santiago de Cuba: **Cine Capitolio** – formerly a barracks in the uprising of 1956. *Victoriano Garzón 256.* **Cine Rialto** – next to the Cathedral. *Félix Pena 654.*

Trinidad: **Cine Romelio Cornelio** – Cuban and some American films. *On Parque Céspedes.*

Dance performances and lessons

It is relatively easy to get dance lessons; just ask at your hotel or *casa particular*. Displays of traditional folk or Afro-

Cuban dance are sometimes given at music venues, but there are also specialist venues for dance.

Havana: **Casa de la Cultura de Plaza** – hosts concerts and shows, including traditional folk and *santería* music, *Calzada, between Calle 6 and Calle 8, Vedado.* **Orestes Dickinson** – gives dance lessons. *San Lázaro 111, 1st Fl., Flat 3, between Crespo and Genios. Tel: 8637359.*

Santiago de Cuba: **Ballet Folkórico Cutatumba** – superb show on Sunday mornings. *Enramada, 2 blocks west of Parque Céspedes.* **Grupo Folklórico del Oriente** – lunchtime and evening shows. *San Francisco and San Félix.*

Trinidad: **Casa Fischer (Artex)** – has nightly shows of Afro-Cuban dance at 9.30pm. *Lino Pérez, between Codania and José Martí.*

The cabaret show at the Tropicana in Havana

Nightclubs

There is a range of nightclubs offering different types of dancing and entertainment. Some are just discos, while others are much grander, offering a cabaret show and live music. Most start late at night with a smart dress code and under 18s are not usually admitted.

Havana: **Casa de la Música** – this has a great reputation with a salsa disco and live bands. *20, corner of 35, Miramar. Tel: 2026147*. **Macumba** – a top Havana disco with a small floor show. *222, corner of 37, La Coronela, La Lisa (in La Giraldilla tourist complex). Tel: 330568*. **El Tropical** – there is a live salsa band most nights; it has an upper section and popular outdoor location. *Salón Rosado Beny Moré, Ave. 41 and 46. Tel: 2061281*. **Tropicana** – hosts perhaps the most famous cabaret shows in the Caribbean, with glamour and prices to match. It is best to go with a tour, bookable at most hotels and tourist offices. *Calle 72 No 4504, between 43 and 45, Marianao. Tel: 2671871*. **Hotel cabarets** – all the main hotels have their own shows, some of which are the same standard as the Tropicana and better value. **Hotel Nacional, Riviera** and **Habana Libre** are all recommended.

Santiago de Cuba: **Tropicana Santiago** – considered one of the best shows on the island. *Autopista Nacional km 1.5. Tel: 68700*. **Hotel discos** – some hotels have lively discos, including the **Santiago** and **Las Américas**.

Trinidad: **Casa de la Música** – daily disco with live performers at weekends. *Plaza Mayor, up the steps past the church*. **Las Cuevas** – merengue and salsa disco in a cave near Hotel Las Cuevas. *Finca Santa Ana. Tel: 996133*.

Music and dance

Perhaps the most authentically Cuban places for music and dance are the *Casas de la Trova* which exist in all Cuban towns. They vary from small, unassuming places which are mainly frequented by locals, to full-blown tourist venues. Most offer traditional live music, specialising in *son* and *bolero*. At some venues, especially the higher-quality ones in cities, you will find Cubans desperate to get in, who will hassle you to pay their entrance fee. Locals will also be keen to dance with you, mostly for sociable reasons although don't be surprised if you find yourself buying the drinks all night! There are also venues offering other types of Cuban music, including *rumba*, *conga* and *charanga*. There is a huge range of music and dance events in Havana. To find out more, look at the listings in the newspapers *Opciones* and *Cartelera*. They are published on Thursdays. In addition, Radio Taíno FM93.3 (an English and Spanish language tourist station) gives regular details of events.

Havana: **Callejón de Hammel** – *rumba* show every Sun from noon–3pm. *Hammel, between Aramburu and Hospital, Centro*.

A rumba performance at Callejón de Hammel in Havana

Casa de la Trova – a small, intimate venue with traditional acoustic music, highly recommended. *San Lázaro, between Belascoaín and Gervasio, Centro. Tel: 8793373.* **Conjunto Folklórico Nacional de Cuba** – *rumba* and Afro-Cuban music every Sat. *Calle 4, between Calzada and 5, Vedado.* **Delirio Habanero** – quality music with great views. *Upstairs on 5th floor of Teatro Nacional, Vedado. Tel: 8784275.* **Jardines del 1830** – top salsa bands play here. *Malecón and Calle 20 beside the road tunnel. Tel: 838309.* **Jazz Café** – live jazz every night, recommended,

SANTIAGO FESTIVALS

There are quite a few festivals in Santiago over the summer. The Festival de Baile (dance festival) takes place 15–19 May; the Festival de Caribe starts first week in July and continues into late July. The Carnival itself is from 18–27 July. Festivals also take place Sept–Dec, including a huge party on New Year's Eve.

on top floor of blue glass building. *Galerías de Paseo, Primera, between Calles A and Paseo, Vedado. Tel: 8383302.* **La Zorra y el Cuervo** – recommended venue for jazz, with

A performance at the Casa de las Tradiciones in Santiago de Cuba

entrance through a British red phone box! *Calle 23, between N and O, Vedado. Tel: 8332402.*

Santiago de Cuba: **Casa de las Tradiciones** – colonial house with loads of atmosphere, good for both listening to live music and for dancing. *Rabí, between José de Diego and García.* **Casa de la Trova** – very popular but touristy upstairs venue overlooking the street. *Heredia 206.* **Casa de los Estudiantes** – a popular venue, in a beautiful building with a patio where bands play. Check in advance what shows are planned. *Heredia, very near Hotel Casa Granda.* **Grupo Folklórico del Oriente** – day and evening dance performances by folk groups. *San Francisco and San Félix.*

Trinidad: **La Canchánchara** – serves a tasty drink of the same name in earthenware pots, and has traditional music at lunchtimes. *Villena 70.* **Casa de la Trova** – good Cuban music in delightful open-air terrace. *One block southeast from the church, just off Plaza Mayor.* Near the Casa de La Trova, you will come across several music venues. Just follow your ear. Most are pretty good. **La Escalinita**, on a balmy terrace to the right of the church, up the steps, has live music at lunchtimes and evenings (part of the Casa de la Música).

Theatre and ballet

The most important venues for theatre, classical music and ballet are all in Havana. There are many festivals held

A statue on the elegant façade of Havana's Gran Teatro

in Havana: see the Festivals section on *pp28–9* for more information.

Amadeo Roldán – marvellously renovated concert hall in which the national and visiting symphony orchestras play. *Calzada and D, Vedado. Tel: 8325551.* **Gran Teatro de La Habana** – Cuban National Ballet and Opera, and Conjunto Folklórico Nacional perform here. *Prado, corner of San Rafael, Centro Habana. Tel: 8613078.* **Teatro Nacional de Cuba** – a complex which holds several auditoriums, hosting all kinds of cultural events and arts festivals. *Paseo, corner of 39, Vedado. Tel: 8796011.*

Children

Children will have a great time in Cuba, not only because there are a lot of sights of interest and activities suitable for them, but also because Cubans love children and you will be treated very well as a result. The family is very important in Cuba and you will make conversation everywhere you go.

Beaches

Beaches are the obvious starting point for families, and there are many lovely beaches, such as Cayo Coco which has shallow, warm water for many metres out to sea. Beach resorts such as Varadero and Guardalavaca are ideal for children, as there are excellent facilities for water sports and for organised activities.

Cities and excursions

Havana is good for children, particularly Habana Vieja, around the Plaza de Armas. There are regular displays of dancing and other activities in the Museo de la Ciudad. The Castillo del Morro and fortification of San Carlos de la Cabaña are also fascinating historical sites which children will enjoy.

They will also appreciate the range of transport options in Havana – after all, how many children from Europe or North America have travelled in a *bicitaxi*, *cocotaxi*, horse-drawn *coche*, or a 1950s Chevrolet?

Excursions from Havana are plentiful, with a variety of tours to the beautiful countryside. The tour to Las Terrazas takes you to an ecological community and natural springs where visitors can swim. A trip to the Viñales Valley should not be missed, either. Learning how tobacco, sugar cane and coffee are grown will fascinate most children.

In Trinidad, there are excursions to nearby Playa Ancón, or a ride on the old steam train that takes you through Valle de los Ingenios to the Iznaga estate tower and farmhouse, where there is a sugar cane press that produces a refreshing juice.

Nature parks

Cuba has developed its wildlife reserves and ecological sites very carefully, with the result that there are many sights where nature and wildlife can be enjoyed. Nature parks include:

Jardín Botánico Soledad, Cienfuegos: a serene and fascinating botanical garden which includes massive Banyan fig trees and an impressive collection of cacti.

Parque Baconao: this is the largest amusement park in Cuba, with a range of attractions that are ideal for children. You can climb up the enormous monolith of Gran Piedra, take a boat trip on Laguna Baconao, spend hours at the children's park of Valle de la Prehistoria with its dinosaur sculptures, visit the excellent aquarium which has regular dolphin shows, and watch rodeo shows at El Oasis. There are also coffee plantations and beaches.

Península de Zapata: the area around Laguna del Tesoro is particularly rich in wildlife and includes the holiday resort of Guamá with its thatched huts, as well as an excellent crocodile farm.

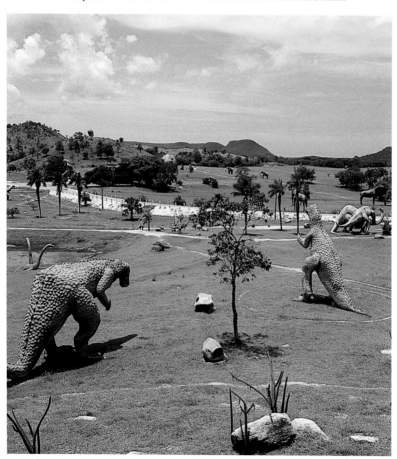

The Valle de la Prehistoria in Parque Baconao

Sport and leisure

Sport plays an important part in life on the island, both for tourists and locals. There is a wide range of outdoor leisure activities available to tourists, such as diving, fishing and sailing. For those who like to watch rather than participate, baseball is the prime spectator sport in Cuba, although there are other options available too.

Sports play a significant role in Cuban cultural life. The national sport is baseball, and many Cubans are glued to the TV or radio when a big league game is on. Over the years, several Cuban baseball stars have managed to defect to the US, to earn untold riches in comparison to the $200 and less per year that they earn at home. Cuba has one of the best baseball teams in the world and, although amateur, is a match for any professional foreign side.

In other sports, standards are high, due to the government-sponsored mass physical education programmes and specialist sporting schools. Cuba is famous on the world stage for athletics, volleyball, basketball and boxing. Sporting legends include Ivan Pedroso, long jump Olympic gold medallist in 2000, Ana Fidelia Quirot, world 800m champion in the mid 1990s, and Javier Sotomayor, high jump gold medallist at the 1992 Olympics in Barcelona.

PARTICIPATORY SPORTS AND LEISURE ACTIVITIES
Caving

There are a number of huge cave systems in Cuba, some of which have been developed for tourists, while others are known only to professional cavers.

The main sites are:

Camagüey – Sierra de Cubitas has several caves containing Amerindian pictographs, such as Los Generales, Las Mercedes, Indio and Pichardo.

Gibara – Tanques Azules, Caletones. The adventure park at Silla de Gibara offers activities such as potholing and cave diving.

Isla de la Juventud – Cuevas de Punta del Este also contains Amerindian pictographs.

Trinidad – Cueva Martín Infierno contains the largest stalagmite in Cuba.

Viñales – Santo Tomás and Cueva del Indio caves.

Zapata Peninsula – there are flooded caves here, which can be dived.

Cycling

Cycling is a great way to see Cuba, as there is an excellent network of tarmac and concrete roads, making most of the country accessible to cyclists. Traffic on the roads is very light, especially out of the main towns, and the scenery can be spectacular. A lot of the roads are in poor condition, with large potholes, but there are plenty of roadside workshops (*talleres*) where repairs can be undertaken.

Some of the bigger hotels and holiday villages have good-quality bicycles for hire, but bear in mind that these will be far superior to the ones that the locals have, many of which were imported from China, so always lock your bike or leave it in a supervised place.

November to May is the best time for cycling in Cuba, and it's best to try to cycle from east to west, in order to avoid the strong northeast trade winds.

For more information, contact: **Blazing Saddles Travels** (*www.cyclecuba.net*) or **Havanatour UK** (*www.havanatour.co.uk*).

Diving

Cuba is one of the best places in the Caribbean for diving, due to its huge coastline (5,700km/3,500 miles), the quantity of small islands (some 4,000),

Cuba is an ideal country for cycling

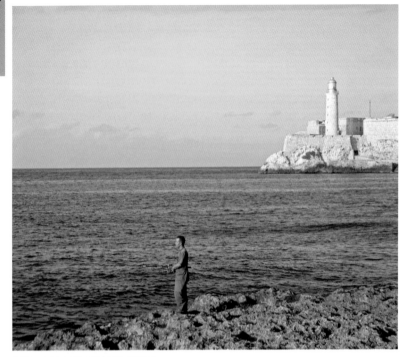

A fisherman on the Malecón, Havana

and the pristine nature of the marine environment.

The main dive areas are: Isla de la Juventud, María La Gorda, Varadero, Archipiélago Jardines del Rey, and the Santiago de Cuba area.

Further information on diving in Cuba can be obtained from:
Cubanacán Nautica, *Calle 184 No 123, Reparto Flores, Havana. Tel: 336675.*
The main company that owns the dive shops (as joint ventures with the Cuban government) is:
Cubanacán (*www.cubanacan.cu*),
See pp141–2 for more information on diving.

Fishing

Ernest Hemingway is credited with popularising fishing in Cuba, and excellent deep-sea and freshwater fishing are available. For freshwater fishing, the *trucha* (largemouth bass) is the most popular catch. Deep-sea fishing can be organised at most marinas in Cuba, although the best facilities are at Marina Hemingway, west of Havana.

Marina Hemingway *Ave. 5 and 248, Santa Fe, Playa, Havana. Tel: 2097270.*
Havanatur Tour and Travel *Edificio Sierra Maestra, Calle 1, between 0 and 2, Playa, Havana. Tel: 2047541.*

Golf

Cuba currently only has two golf courses, although ten more are being built in many of the tourist areas.

The nine-hole **Club de Golf Habana** welcomes non-members and costs CUC30 for 18 holes. Equipment can be hired and lessons are available. Other sporting facilities include swimming pool, squash and tennis courts, billiards and a bowling alley.
Carretera de Vento km 8, Capdevila, Boyeros (towards the airport). Tel: 649918.

The **Club de Golf Las Américas** in Varadero has been upgraded in recent years from 9 holes to 18 holes, the original course being laid out around the mansion of the Dupont family, now the *Mansión Xanadú*, built in the 1920s. The facilities are good, with putting greens, a chipping green and a driving range, as well as lessons and hire equipment offered. Packages of a few days are available with accommodation in the clubhouse.
Avenida las Américas, Varadero. Tel: 668482. www.varaderogolfclub.com. Open daily, make reservations 24 hours in advance, through tour desks or directly through the club.

Horse riding

Horse riding is a popular activity for travellers wanting to spend time in the countryside, especially in the Viñales Valley. In many ecotourist centres, resorts and camping areas there are horse-riding facilities available.

There is a riding centre in Havana. It costs around CUC3 per hour with guide included. There is no need to reserve, just turn up. The centre is well run and horses are well looked after. **El Rodeo** – *Parque Lenin (near the Las Ruinas restaurant), Havana.*

Hunting

The country has a number of hunting reserves (*cotos de caza*) where people are allowed to hunt birds and small animals under the supervision of forest rangers. Many lodges for freshwater fishing also have hunting facilities. There are no specialist hunting agencies but more information can be obtained from **Havanatur Tour and Travel** *Edificio Sierra Maestra, Calle 1, between 0 and 2, Playa, Havana. Tel: 2047541.*

Sailing

The island is an ideal stopping-off point for yachts and sailing boats, and there is a good selection of marinas offering moorings, boat rental and other services. Most sailing is done around the Archipiélago de los Canarreos, while the best time of the year for sailing is from December to April, when the weather is mild.

The biggest marina is the **Marina Hemingway** *Ave. 5 and 248, Santa Fe, Playa, Havana. Tel: 2097270.* **Puertosol** owns many of the tourist marinas: *Vía Blanca km 18, Playa Tarará, Havana. Tel: 971462.*

Golf at a course in Boyeros (towards Havana airport)

SPECTATOR SPORTS

Baseball and boxing are by far the most popular sports in Cuba, but volleyball, basketball, athletics and football are also widespread. After the Revolution, professional sports were abolished and big investments were made in amateur sports and in physical education in general. Cuba has some outstanding teams, particularly in baseball, boxing, volleyball, athletics, weightlifting and water polo. For more information on sports in Cuba, contact **Cubadeportes SA** *Calle 20 No 710, between 7 and 9, Playa, Havana. Tel: 2022443. www.cubadeportes.cu*

The main venue for watching sports in Cuba is the **Ciudad Deportiva** ('Sports City') in Havana. Built in 1958, it is enclosed by a dome and seats 18,000 spectators. It hosts a wide range of sports, from volleyball and basketball to martial arts and table tennis. International sporting events are usually sold out. Attending is highly recommended due to the great

atmosphere and cheap entrance fee, only a few Cuban pesos. There are limited food and drink facilities, so remember to take your own.
Ave. de la Independencia and Vía Blanca, Havana. Tel: 545000.
Buy tickets at the venue in advance.

The following stadiums also regularly host sporting competitions:
Estadio Panamericano *Carretera de Cojímar km 1.5, just outside Havana. Tel: 954140.* Swimming, water polo, football, athletics and baseball.
Sala Polivalente Ramón Fonst *Ave. de la Independencia and Bruzón, Havana. Tel: 8811011.* Volleyball and basketball.

Baseball

Cubans have a great passion for their national game, which first developed in the late 19th century as a symbol of national identity and anti-colonialism. The official baseball season is from November to March, culminating in the national play-offs. There are regular games on some weekday evenings and at weekends. Games can last up to three hours, although this doesn't seem to dull the spectators' fanaticism! Tickets for games cost a few pesos and can be purchased at the stadium box office just before the game. The best place to see major league baseball is the Estadio Panamericano (*see above*). Built in the 1950s, it is home to two teams, the Industriales (Los Azules)

and the Metropolitanos, and seats 55,000 spectators.

Boxing

Cuba has one of the best boxing teams in the world, winning many Olympic titles. Fights can be seen in Havana at *Coliseo de la Ciudad Deportiva, Ave. de la Independencia, corner of Vía Blanca. Tel: 6485000.*

Cycling

Havana's professional racetrack is at the **Velódromo Reinaldo Paseiro**, part of the Estadio Panamericano, on the south side of the Vía Blanca. Cuba hosts several international competitions, including *Vuelta a Cuba* in February. For more information, contact the **Federación Cubana de Ciclismo** in Habana del Este. *Tel: 973776.*

Kayaking at Cayo Coco beach

Food and drink

The quality and range of food in Cuba have improved a great deal in recent years, and there is much more fresh produce available. However, visitors expecting new culinary experiences and haute cuisine will be disappointed. Drinking in Cuba, however, is a highly pleasurable experience, with rum taking centre stage on the alcoholic front, and with a range of fruit juices and other packaged drinks available, too.

What to eat

Traditional Cuban food is known as *cocina criolla* and is based on a mixture of Spanish, African and Colombian Indian influences. It is rarely spicy. The national dish is roast pork with *congrís* (rice mixed with black beans) and *yuca* (cassava) or fried plantain. Main dishes mainly consist of rice and beans with either chicken or pork, with a salad of tomatoes and cucumber. Fish and seafood are good, too. The main soup, *potaje*, is made from black or red beans, garlic, onion, pepper, powdered cumin and pork. Another soup is *ajiaco*, a kind of minestrone made with a variety of vegetables and meat.

The choice for vegetarians is very limited, although pizzas, salads, omelettes and cheese sandwiches are available, but be aware that beans and rice are often cooked in meat fat. However, with advance warning, your restaurant or *casa particular* will prepare proper vegetarian food.

There is a magnificent range of fresh fruit, and, depending on the season, mango, guava, papaya and pineapple are available. Cubans are big fans of ice cream, and there are often queues at ice cream parlours, especially at *Coppelia*.

What to drink

Rum is the national drink and forms the basis of most cocktails. There is a huge range available (*see pp50–51*).

Beer is pretty good, the most common brands being Cristal, a light beer, and Bucanero, stronger and very popular in Santiago de Cuba. Hatuey beer is also available, especially in Havana. Cuba does produce wine, but it is not particularly good. Imported wines, especially from Chile, are a better bet.

There are delicious fresh fruit drinks, as well as shakes (called *batidos*), using fresh papaya, mango, pineapple and oranges. The most common fruit squash is lemonade, made with lime, sugar, water and ice. Also highly recommended is *guarapo*, made from fresh sugar cane (it isn't as sweet as you might think!). Canned soft drinks are called *refrescos*, while fruit juices can be bought in cartons and are very popular. Try the *guayaba* (guava) flavour if you want something a little different.

Cuban coffee is very strong. It is often sold in tiny cups and sometimes has sugar already added. Teas are also available, especially camomile (*manzanilla*).

Where to eat

The standard is much higher in international-class hotels than in state-run restaurants. One of the advantages of staying in *casas particulares* is that the home-cooking is often excellent, with huge portions, and your hosts are often able to buy all sorts of ingredients in private or black markets. They may or may not have government licences to serve food to their guests.

State-owned restaurants vary hugely in quality, but some may be quite good. Do not expect authentic dishes if you eat at restaurants offering international cuisine. Resort hotels tend to offer buffet meals as part of the 'all-inclusive' package. Private restaurants are called *paladares* and often consist of a handful of tables with a limited range of dishes. *Paladares* open and shut frequently, depending on the government's policy at the time for giving out licences. Visitors are often approached in the street and offered to be shown to a *paladar*, which may or may not have the required government licence.

Snacks and fast food can be found in the streets of most towns. Small pizzas are normally filling and good value. The American-style fast-food chain El Rápido offers safe but bland fare.

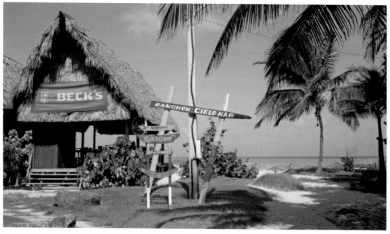

A beachside restaurant at Varadero

Food and drink

In the restaurant listings below, star ratings indicate the average cost of a meal per person, excluding drinks.

★   Less than CUC10
★★   CUC10–25
★★★   CUC25–45
★★★★   More than CUC45

HAVANA

Havana has the biggest choice of restaurants with the highest quality of ingredients, but costs are higher than in other cities.

Al Medina ★
Arab food in lovely colonial mansion.
Oficios 12, between Obrapía and Obispo, Habana Vieja.
Tel: 8671041. Open: noon–midnight.

Dominica ★★
Very smart Italian restaurant with vegetarian options.
O'Reilly 108, corner of Mercaderes, Habana Vieja. Tel: 8662918.

El Floridita ★★★
Sumptuous décor, and a favourite haunt of Hemingway (a stool in the corner of the bar is kept empty in his honour).
Corner of Obispo and Monserrate, next to

Parque Central, Habana Vieja. Tel: 8671299.
Open: noon–10pm

La Paella ★★
The best paella in Havana, in a charming setting.
Oficios, between Lamparilla and Obrapía, Habana Vieja.
Open: noon–10pm.

El Tocororo ★★★★
Excellent food including ostrich steak, in colonial mansion with terrace.
Calle 18 and Av 3.
Tel: 2042209. Open: Mon–Sat noon–midnight.

La Torre ★★
Best French food in Havana, with great views.
Calles 17 and M, at top of Edificio Fosca, Vedado. Tel: 8327306. Open: noon–midnight.

WESTERN CENTRAL CUBA
Trinidad

Don Antonio ★
Good Creole restaurant, with fish a speciality.
Calle Izquierdo 118, between Bolívar and Guinart. Tel: 96548. Open: noon–10pm.

El Jigüe ★★
Good food and atmosphere, often with live music.

Maceo 402, corner of Colón. Tel: 94316.
Open: noon–10pm.

Plaza Mayor ★★
Elegant setting with buffet lunch and dinner available.
Calle Real 15, corner of Rosario. Tel: 6470.
Open: noon–11pm.

Sol y Son ★
Pleasant 19th-century house with courtyard. Vegetarian options.
Simón Bolívar 283, between País and Martí.
Open: 7pm–midnight.

Varadero
Las Américas, Mansión Xanadú ★★★★
This is wonderful dining in the classy old Dupont mansion overlooking the beach at Varadero. Seafood and great wine.
Autopista Sur km 7. Tel: 667750. Open: noon–10.30pm.

El Bodegón Criollo ★★
This lovely restaurant with outside seating, overlooking the sea at Varadero, serves up solid Cuban dishes and seafood platters, too.
Avenida Playa, corner of Calle 40. Tel: 667784.
Open: noon–11pm.

SANTIAGO DE CUBA

La Maison ★

Eat in the patio restaurant or outdoor cafeteria of this white neoclassical Reparto Vista Alegre mansion. Chicken, steak and lobster feature.
Avenida Manduley, between Calles 1 and 3. Tel: 641117. Open: patio noon–midnight, cafeteria 9am–1am.

Restaurante El Morro ★★

Dine on a set menu of soup, beef, prawns, salad, dessert and coffee in a spectacular setting overlooking the castle and the sea.
Castillo del Morro. Open: noon–4pm.

Roof Garden, Casa Granda ★★

Enjoy seafood skewers or minute steak with a wonderful view of the cathedral and bay.
Calle Heredia 201, facing Parque Céspedes. Tel: 686600. Open: 11am–1am.

La Taberna de Dolores ★

Good value Spanish food in a large patio.
Aguilera, corner of Reloj. Tel: 623913.

Where to drink

Most bars in Cuba have live music. Most will be visited by groups of musicians who play for 15 minutes and then gather tips and try to sell their CDs before moving on. Music venues will have a more structured evening of music. We have detailed only the best or most popular bars in the major cities.

HAVANA

Bar El Louvre

A great place to watch the sun going down over Parque Central.
At Hotel Inglaterra, Prado 416. Tel: 8608595.

La Bodeguita del Medio

Perhaps the most popular with tourists in Havana, because of its links to Hemingway. Always crowded.
Empedrado 207, close to the Cathedral. Tel: 8668857

Casa de la Amistad

Peaceful, with a beautiful garden extension.
Paseo 406, Vedado. Tel: 8303114.

Habana Café

A very popular 1950s themed venue.

Entrance to the left of main entrance of Hotel Meliá Cohiba, Paseo, between Calles 1 and 3. Tel: 8333636.

Hotel Sevilla

Nice courtyard with fountain. Popular with Graham Greene fans.
Trocadero 55 and Prado. Tel: 8608560.

TRINIDAD

Bar Las Ruinas de Segarte

Pleasant bar in ruined courtyard.
Menéndez, between Márquez and Galdós.

Palenque de los Congos Reales

An excellent courtyard venue with Afro-Cuban performances.
Echerri, near Francisco Yavier Zerquera.

SANTIAGO DE CUBA

La Terraza

Great people-watching venue overlooking Parque Céspedes.
Casa Granda, Calle Heredia 201.

Las Columnitas

Outdoor bar and café.
One block from Enramada, San Félix and Callejón del Carmen.

Food and drink

Hotels and accommodation

There is an increasing choice of accommodation in Cuba, and standards have risen dramatically since 1980 when the country opened its doors to foreign visitors. While Cuba is focusing much of its efforts on attracting the package-holiday tourist to its beach resorts, as well as upmarket tourists to its cities, there is still plenty available for other types of traveller.

Casas particulares

The most authentic and rewarding place to stay is in a *casa particular*, private accommodation offered by Cuban families who rent up to two spare rooms in their home. They are often spotlessly clean, with great hospitality and are recognisable by a sticker on the front door with two blue chevrons on a white background, and '*Arrendador Inscripto*' written on it.

Hotels

The hotel sector is growing quickly, with all hotels being majority owned by the government. The best hotels are those with foreign management or foreign investment, and most have 4 or 5 stars. There are some mid-range, Cuban-owned hotels built in the 1950s, but they are often run-down and below international standards.

It is important to book your first night's accommodation well in advance of travelling, especially during the peak season of December to February.

Visitors will need to fill in any hotel name and address on their Tourist Card before travelling to Cuba, otherwise this may cause delays or problems on arrival.

Price guides

The price categories below will give you a rough idea of the kind of accommodation in each price range:

Less than CUC30 ★
For this budget, it is far better to stay in *casas particulares* than in hotels. They are often attractive colonial homes with original furnishings, courtyards and very comfortable character rooms, some with en-suite bathrooms. Your hosts will almost always offer breakfast and sometimes evening meals. Often the food served is much tastier than in a state restaurant. It is likely you will be given your own key to the house.

CUC40–100 ★★
This is the lower end of the state hotel sector and some hotels in this

price category will not have been recently renovated. Fixtures and fittings may well be outdated or basic. In the countryside, hotels may be much more attractive than their city counterparts.

CUC100–150 ★★★

Hotels in this category will be very high quality, with good facilities and furnishings. Some may be small, intimate and charming.

More than CUC150 ★★★★

These are international-standard hotels. Many of the beach resorts are not particularly attractively designed but those in cities are often in very pretty restored buildings.

HAVANA

Casa del Científico ★★

Adequately equipped rooms in this wonderful building, the former home of President José Gómez.
Calle Prado 212, corner of Trocadero. Tel: 8621607.

Chez Nous ★

The friendly owners make you feel welcome in their beautiful *casa*. There's also a rooftop patio.
Calle Brasil 115, between Cuba and San Ignacio. Tel: 8626287.
cheznous@ceniai.inf.cu

Hotel Ambos Mundos ★★★

In downtown Havana, this smart hotel is an attractive place to stay. The lobby bar with live piano music and Roof Garden are always busy.

Calle Obispo, corner of Mercaderes. Tel: 8609530.
comercial@habaguanexhamundos.cu

Hotel Nacional de Cuba ★★★★

This 1930s hotel is the grandest in Cuba and sits on a promontory facing the entire Malecón. Rooms are comfortable and well equipped.
Calle O, corner of 21, Vedado. Tel: 8733564.
www.hotelnacionaldecuba.cu

Hotel Santa Isabel ★★★★

A charming and luxurious hotel in a converted Spanish colonial mansion. Rooms are delightful; the hotel has many facilities and staff are friendly.
Calle Baratillo 9, between Obispo and Narciso López. Tel: 8608201.
comercial@habaguanexhsisabel.co.cu

Hotel Saratoga ★★★★

This luxurious and elegant hotel has an unbeatable view from its superb roof terrace, complete with swimming pool. Rooms are extremely comfortable.
Calle Prado 603, corner of Dragones. Tel: 8681000. www.hotel-saratoga.com

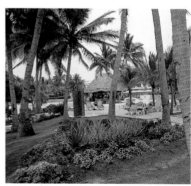

A typical all-inclusive hotel resort in Varadero

Jorge Potts ★

This modern, ground-floor *casa* is run by a friendly and welcoming couple. The rooms are quiet and well furnished. *Apto 11, Calle I No 456, between Calle 21 and 23. Tel: 8329032. www.havanaroomrental.com*

Mesón de la Flota ★★

Characterful rooms with spacious bathrooms and lovely balconies. Also has a popular restaurant. *Calle Mercaderes 257, between Brasil and Amargura. Tel: 8629281.*

WESTERN CUBA

Hotel Los Jazmines ★★

Just outside the village of Viñales, with a lovely pool on a terrace that has a spectacular view. Rooms, in the main colonial building or in *cabañas*, are adequate. *Carretera a Viñales. Tel: 796205.*

WESTERN CENTRAL CUBA

Hostal Florida Center ★

The gregarious Angel runs this gorgeous *casa particular* in Santa Clara, stuffed full of antiques and with a cooling, plant-filled courtyard. *Calle Maestra Nicolasa 56 (Candelaria), between Colón and Maceo. Tel: 208161.*

Hotel Tryp Península Varadero ★★★★

Two-storey villas in plantation style surrounded by luscious gardens, with two pools (one for children) and the beach nearby. *Parque Nacional Hicacos, Varadero. Tel: 668800. www.tryp-peninsulavaradero.com*

Trinidad

Casa Muñoz ★

A wonderful colonial *casa*. The owner is a photographer and runs workshops for interested visitors. *Calle José Martí 401, between Fidel Claro and Santiago Escobar. Tel: 93673. http://casa.trinidadphoto.com*

Grand Hotel ★★★

The only hotel in central Trinidad, but very comfortable. Some rooms have balconies with views over the park. *Calle José Martí 252, corner of Lino Pérez. Tel: 96077. www.iberostar.com*

EASTERN CENTRAL CUBA

Hotel Colón ★★

This small, slightly old-fashioned hotel in Camagüey has small but well-furnished rooms and large public areas. *Calle República 472, between San José and San Martín. Tel: 283346. www.islazul.cu*

Hotel Meliá Cayo Guillermo ★★★★

This luxury resort on a lovely beach offers a variety of activities including diving and horse riding. Rooms are comfortable and well equipped. *Jardines del Rey, Cayo Guillermo, Ciego de Ávila. Tel: 301680. www.solmeliacuba.com*

Hotel Paradisus Río de Oro ★★★★

An upmarket hotel with several exclusive beaches, a large swimming pool, a spa, some excellent à la carte restaurants and very comfortable rooms.

Playa Esmeralda, Careterra
Guardalavaca, Rafael Freyre, Holguín.
Tel: 30090. www.paradisus-riodeoro.com
Los Vitrales ★
An extremely friendly family has two
comfortable rooms in a former convent
in Camagüey.
Calle Avellaneda 3, between Calle
General Gómez and Martí. Tel: 295866.
requejobarreto@gmail.com

SANTIAGO DE CUBA
Casa Maruchi ★
This lovely colonial *casa* has a friendly
owner and is decorated with plants.
It has two comfortable rooms.
San Félix 357, between Trinidad
and San Germán.

Tel: 620767.
maruchi@infomeil.com
Hotel Casa Granda ★★★
A handsome cream building with roof
and café terraces boasts some of the
best views in the city.
Calle Heredia 201, facing
Parque Céspedes. Tel: 686600.
comercia@casagran.gca.tur.cu

EASTERN CUBA
Hotel El Castillo ★★
A small hotel in Baracoa in an elevated
position. The terrace, with swimming
pool, has views across the town and
over the sea.
Calle Calixto García, Reparto Paraíso.
Tel: 45195. www.gaviota-grupo.com

Hotels and accommodation

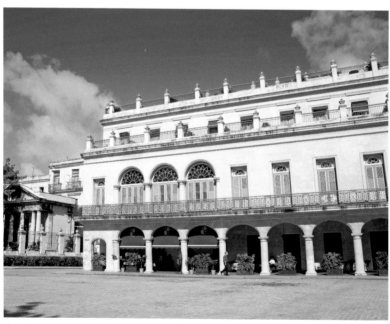

The elegant Hotel Santa Isabel in Habana Vieja

Practical guide

Arrival

By air

Havana is the main international airport in Cuba, although there are several others classed as international, including Varadero. The international terminal at Havana airport includes shops, exchange facilities and snack bars. Immigration can be slow, especially at night. There are no hotels at the airport, so visitors will need to take a taxi to the city, which will cost CUC20–25. There is an accommodation desk at the airport if you need to book a last-minute hotel.

Formalities

The requirements and documents asked for by the Cuban immigration authorities are a valid passport, a return ticket, and a Tourist Card (*tarjeta de turista*). Tourist Cards are valid for 30 days and are solely for visits of a tourist nature. They can be issued by the travel agency or airline from whom you bought your air ticket, or a Cuban consulate. You will need to fill in your personal data and state where you are planning to stay in Cuba (often the name of the hotel where you are staying on your first night). Tourist Cards can

The José Martí airport in Havana

be extended for another 30 days by going to the Immigration Office in certain cities in Cuba.

Special regulations apply for holders of US passports. American law makes it illegal for US passport holders to spend money in Cuba, and thus travel to Cuba, but it is possible to obtain a licence from the US Treasury Department if the trip is for religious or humanitarian trips or for freelance journalists or university students. Some US travellers visit Cuba by travelling via Canada, Mexico or the Caribbean and thus cover their tracks. (NB: Cuban immigration do not stamp passports.)

Visitors for non-tourist reasons, such as business people, journalists, students, and nationals of countries without a visa-free agreement with Cuba, should check visa requirements. An official/business visa may be required.

Camping

There are official campsites all over Cuba, although they are mainly used by Cubans on holiday. They mostly consist of basic cabins, although some are designed for tourists with camper vans. The main agency to arrange bookings and transport for camping is **Cubamar**, based in Havana at *Paseo 306, between 13 and 15, Vedado*. In addition, each major town will have a Campismo office for access to local campsites.

Children

Children should experience no real problems in Cuba, but sensible

CUBA

☂ May to November
☀ December to April

WEATHER CONVERSION CHART

25.4mm = 1 inch
°F = 1.8 × °C + 32

precautions should be taken. The sun is very strong, so protection in the form of a hat and strong sunscreen are required, and lots of bottled water should be drunk. Remember to take a supply of toilet paper, as public toilets are generally hard to find and often very dirty. Wet wipes and antiseptic hand cream are also very useful.

The most common health problems for children are diarrhoea and vomiting. To avoid this, it is best to avoid ice in drinks, and food or drinks sold on the street. The treatment of diarrhoea is the same as for adults but should start earlier and be more intensive.

Climate

Cuba has a moderate subtropical climate, due to its location under the

CONVERSION TABLE

FROM	TO	MULTIPLY BY
Inches	Centimetres	2.54
Feet	Metres	0.3048
Yards	Metres	0.9144
Miles	Kilometres	1.6090
Acres	Hectares	0.4047
Gallons	Litres	4.5460
Ounces	Grams	28.35
Pounds	Grams	453.6
Pounds	Kilograms	0.4536
Tons	Tonnes	1.0160

To convert back, for example from centimetres to inches, divide by the number in the third column.

MEN'S SUITS

UK	36	38	40	42	44	46	48
Rest of Europe	46	48	50	52	54	56	58
USA	36	38	40	42	44	46	48

DRESS SIZES

UK	8	10	12	14	16	18
France	36	38	40	42	44	46
Italy	38	40	42	44	46	48
Rest of Europe	34	36	38	40	42	44
USA	6	8	10	12	14	16

MEN'S SHIRTS

UK	14	14.5	15	15.5	16	16.5	17
Rest of Europe	36	37	38	39/40	41	42	43
USA	14	14.5	15	15.5	16	16.5	17

MEN'S SHOES

UK	7	7.5	8.5	9.5	10.5	11
Rest of Europe	41	42	43	44	45	46
USA	8	8.5	9.5	10.5	11.5	12

WOMEN'S SHOES

UK	4.5	5	5.5	6	6.5	7
Rest of Europe	38	38	39	39	40	41
USA	6	6.5	7	7.5	8	8.5

Tropic of Cancer, with warm temperatures and an average of 330 days of sun per year. There are two seasons: the rainy season (May to November) and the dry season (December to April).

The summer months of June to September are warmer and sunnier than the rest of the year, with average summer temperatures of 25°C (77°F). The winter average is 22°C (71.6°F). The day and night temperatures differ less in the coastal regions than they do inland.

Due to its long and narrow shape on an east–west axis, Cuba experiences refreshing trade winds and sea breezes. Santiago de Cuba on the southeast corner is the exception to this, being several degrees warmer than the rest of the island. The eastern part of the country is generally warmer than the west. The water temperature is usually around 25°C (77°F).

Conversion tables

Clothing sizes are usually given in US or European measurements, depending on the origin of the item.

Crime

Compared to most other countries in Latin America, Cuba is very safe. Travellers will find that they are able to walk around most areas of Havana and other cities at any time of the day, without feeling ill at ease. Punishments for crimes against tourists are severe. However, the level of petty crime is

A horse-drawn carriage in Plaza de San Francisco in Habana Vieja

increasing, mainly due to the growing number of tourists on the island and the large financial gains available, and there have been reported cases of robberies, especially pickpocketing or bag snatching. Remember, Cuba is a poor country where the average salary is about CUC10-12 per month.

Leave your valuables, documents and money in the hotel safe. Do not carry all your money with you in the same place. If carrying a day-rucksack, hold it in front of you when in crowded places, especially bars. Take some of your money as traveller's cheques (not American Express). Do not wear showy jewellery or have your camera too visible. If you hire a car, park near hotels or in pay car parks wherever possible, and do not leave any belongings visible in the car.

Customs regulations

You are allowed to take personal items and medicines into Cuba, plus extra non-commercial items whose overall value is no more than CUC1,000 (subject to duty). It is forbidden to import fresh food or plants, as well as explosives, drugs or pornography.

In terms of duty-free allowances, you can bring in a maximum of 200 cigarettes or 50 cigars or 250g (9oz) of loose tobacco, and 3 litres (0.66 gallons) of wine or other alcoholic beverages, if you are over 18.

If you intend to take more than 50 cigars out of the country, you must produce a receipt of their purchase at a state-run shop. To take works of art out of the country, you must have an official stamp, available from most art shops and stalls.

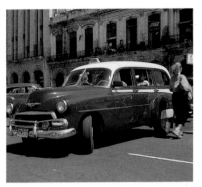

The 1950s taxis in Havana are intended for locals only

Avoid buying items made from protected or endangered species such as tortoiseshell, black coral or bags or belts made from non-farmed reptile skins. These are covered under the Convention on International Trade in Endangered Species (CITES). See *www.advana.co.cu*

Driving
Car hire
Car hire is relatively expensive, especially when adding in the cost of petrol, although it is an increasingly popular way to see the island, and fly-drive packages are available from abroad. To hire a car while in Cuba, tourists must have a driver's licence from their home country or an international licence, be over 21 years of age and be able to show their passport to the car rental company. The main companies include **Transautos** and **Havanautos**, which have good support networks, and many airports and large hotels will have a car

rental desk. Try to ensure that the car is filled with fuel to avoid having to search for a petrol station on your first day.

Driving
Travelling by car is an excellent way to see the island, especially out of the major cities. Roads will be relatively empty, although traffic is increasing as the economy picks up. The condition of the roads is variable, although *autopistas* are mostly fairly good. Towns often have a lot of potholes in the streets. It is best to keep your speed down, even on *autopistas*, as there are often slow-moving vehicles on the road.

In the summer, it is best to drive in the mornings to avoid the hottest part of the day. Many Cubans hitch-hike and a lift will be appreciated, although you are not obliged to pick up hitch-hikers. It is not advisable to travel at night, as lighting is very poor and there will be people and animals walking on the road. Signposting is mostly very poor, so you may well need to ask for directions in many areas.

Fuel
Petrol is available to foreigners in Cupet stations, payable in CUC. There are not many stations outside the main towns, so it is best to fill up wherever possible, well before the tank gets empty. Many car-hire companies will be able to give you a free copy of an *automapa* which shows locations of stations across the island.

Parking
Park in supervised car parks or near hotels wherever possible. Thefts of wheels from hire cars or belongings from cars are not uncommon.

Traffic regulations
In Cuba, traffic drives on the right. The speed limit is 20km/h (12mph) in parking areas, 50km/h (31mph) in towns, 60km/h (37mph) on dirt roads, 90km/h (56mph) on asphalt roads and 100km/h (62mph) on *autopistas*. Seat belts are often only fitted on more modern cars and are not compulsory. In general, the police are fairly tolerant with tourists. It is common practice to sound the horn when overtaking a lorry or before making a sharp turn.

Electricity
The electricity supply is 110 or 220 volts AC, 60 Hz, with flat-pinned plug sockets. Many recently-built hotels have 220-volt currents, but the most usual is 110 volts (same as in the USA). For visitors with European-style appliances, it is a good idea to buy a voltage converter before travelling.

Embassies
Canada
Calle 30 No 518, corner of Ave. 7, Miramar, Havana. Tel: 2042516.
United Kingdom and Northern Ireland
Calle 34 No 702–4, corner of Ave. 7, Miramar, Havana. Tel: 2041771.

People waiting at a bus stop in Habana Vieja

Language

BASIC		NUMBERS	
hello	hola	0	cero
goodbye	adiós	1	uno (m), una (f)
yes	sí	2	dos
no	no	3	tres
friend	amigo (m), amiga (f)	4	cuatro
thank you	gracias	5	cinco
Where is the bathroom?	¿Dónde está el baño?	6	seis
		7	siete
COURTESY		8	ocho
please	por favor	9	nueve
thank you	gracias	10	diez
you're welcome	de nada	20	veinte
sorry	disculpe	30	treinta
excuse me	perdón	40	cuarenta
it doesn't matter	no importa	50	cincuenta
		60	sesenta
GREETINGS		70	setenta
How are you?	¿Cómo estás?	80	ochenta
Very well, thank you	Muy bien, gracias	90	noventa
Good day, good morning	Buenos días	100	cien
Good afternoon	Buenas tardes	200	doscientos
Good night	Buenas noches	300	trescientos
How's it going?	¿Cómo te va?	400	cuatrocientos
What's happening?	¿Qué pasa?	500	quinientos
What's your name?	¿Cómo te llamas?	600	seiscientos
Welcome	Bienvenido	700	setecientos
		800	ochocientos
CHANGING MONEY		900	novecientos
Where can I change dollars?	¿Dónde puedo cambiar dólares?	1,000	mil
traveller's cheques	cheques de viajero		
Is the bank open?	¿El banco está abierto?		
How much is the dollar worth?	¿A cómo está el dólar?		
Do you need identification?	¿Necesita identificación?		
Where do I sign?	¿Dónde firmo?		
May I have some large and small bills?	¿Puede darme billetes grandes y chicos?		
the rest in change?	¿el resto en cambio?		

APPROACHING SOMEONE FOR HELP

Excuse me, sir	Perdón, señor
ma'am	señora
miss/ms	señorita
Do you speak English?	¿Habla usted inglés?
I'm sorry	Lo siento
I don't speak Spanish	No hablo español
Please speak more slowly	Hable más despacio, por favor
Please repeat	Repita, por favor
May I ask a question?	¿Una pregunta, por favor?
Could you please help me?	¿Podría ayudarme?
Where is ...?	¿Dónde está ...?
Thank you very much	Muchas gracias

PAYING THE BILL

The bill, please	La cuenta, por favor
How much do I owe you?	¿Cuánto le debo?
Is service included?	¿El servicio está incluido?
This is for you	Esto es para usted

EATING

bread	pan
butter	mantequilla
coffee	café
fork	tenedor
knife	cuchillo
napkin	servilleta
pepper	pimienta
plate	plato
salt	sal
spoon	cuchara
tea	té
water	agua

DAYS OF THE WEEK

Sunday	domingo
Monday	lunes
Tuesday	martes
Wednesday	miércoles
Thursday	jueves
Friday	viernes
Saturday	sábado

MONTHS OF THE YEAR

January	enero
February	febrero
March	marzo
April	abril
May	mayo
June	junio
July	julio
August	agosto
September	septiembre
October	octubre
November	noviembre
December	diciembre

DIRECTIONS

left	izquierda
right	derecha
far	lejos
near	cerca
street	calle
avenue	avenida
north	norte
south	sur
east	este
west	oeste

US Interests Section
Calle Calzada, between L & M, Vedado, Havana.
Tel: 333551 or 333543.

Emergency telephone numbers

Asistur: *Calle Prado 208, between Colón and Trocadero, Havana. Tel: 8664499. www.asistur.cu*
Asistur Santiago: *202 Calle 4, between 7 and 9, Centro de Negocios, Reparto Vista. Tel: 686128.*
Ambulance and First Aid: *Havana 8381185.*
Police: *Havana 867777; Santiago 226116.*
Fire Brigade: *Havana 105; Santiago 226115.*

Health

Cuba should pose no unusual health risks: the country has an excellent health system and there are not many tropical diseases, meaning that no vaccinations or inoculations are required. Visitors travelling in rural areas in rough conditions may wish to consider vaccinations for typhoid, polio, tetanus and hepatitis A. Insect repellent is recommended, especially if you are visiting wetlands or swamp areas. However, everyday pharmaceutical items are in short supply so it is best to bring your own supply of pain relievers, antibiotics, stomach treatments and so on.

Around 95 per cent of hotels have a doctor on the premises for the provision of primary care to patients. In addition, there are eight international clinics that offer specialist treatment in Pinar del Río, Varadero, Cienfuegos, Trinidad, Cayo Coco, Santa Lucía, Guardalavaca and Santiago de Cuba. Payment is in dollars, and medicines can be bought here.

Health regulations are only applicable to travellers from countries where there is endemic yellow fever and cholera, or countries declared infected areas by the WHO, in which case an International Vaccination Certificate is required. It is advisable for all tourists travelling to Cuba to take out health insurance.

The most common health problem in Cuba is diarrhoea and vomiting, caused by stomach bugs or food poisoning, and the usual treatments of rest, fluid and salt replacement are recommended. To avoid these problems, it is best to avoid ice in drinks, and food or drinks sold on the street. Cuba is relatively humid, so visitors are likely to feel tired and apathetic for the first few days. Remember to drink lots of bottled water; avoid the tap water.

Insurance

Make sure you have adequate travel insurance before you travel, and always read the small print. All losses must be reported to the police and/or hotel authorities within 24 hours and a written report obtained for insurance purposes. This may be difficult to obtain but it is necessary.

When hiring a car, two optional insurances are available. The first covers accidents but not theft, and the second covers all risks except for the loss of a tyre. In the event of an accident, a copy of the police report must be obtained to show the car-hire company.

Internet

Internet access is increasingly available to foreigners in Cuba, although very few Cubans gain access to the web. Pre-paid cards are available from the ETECSA phone company which allow access for a set number of hours. The main locations for internet access in Havana are the Capitolio and the Hotel Inglaterra. Major hotels also have internet access but these tend to be more expensive. Other major tourist towns in Cuba tend to have at least one internet café.

Lost property

To report the loss or theft of personal documents or belongings, go to the nearest police station or find a police officer. You may have to wait a long time to make your report. Remember to take a photocopy of the main sections of your passport, in case you lose the original.

Maps

Maps are usually very good in Cuba and more up to date than those bought abroad. One of the recommended maps is the *Mapa Geográfico* (Ediciones GEO). The best map for drivers is the *Guía de Carreteras* (Road Guide), which is very accurate. Maps can be bought at tourist offices and major hotels. In Havana a good shop for maps is **El Navegante**, *Mercaderes, between Obispo and Oficios.*

Media

The leading daily newspaper in Cuba is *Granma,* which has a weekly international version published in English, French, Portuguese and Spanish called *Granma International.* Internet versions can be found at *www.granma.cu.* There is a business monthly paper on investments in Cuba, *Business Tips on Cuba.*

There are two national TV channels, Cubavisión and Tele Rebelde, while there are several national, municipal and regional radio stations. Many hotels have a satellite dish with CNN in Spanish or English, and some broadcast a TV channel especially for tourists.

Money matters
Credit cards

All hotels and many restaurants and shops will accept payment by credit card, as long as it is not issued in the USA. Any problems using credit cards should be reported to the Centro de Tarjetas de Crédito in Havana. However, it is important to carry a certain amount of cash to pay for smaller purchases.

Currency

The Cuban peso (*moneda nacional*) is the national currency. There are notes of 1, 3, 5, 10, 20, 50 and 100 pesos, as well as coins equivalent to 1 and 3 pesos. There are coins of 1, 2, 5 and 20 cents.

Most products available to tourists are paid for in Cuban Convertible Pesos (CUC). A ban on the dollar enacted by Castro in 2004 in retaliation against increased trade restrictions imposed by the USA means it is no longer legal tender in Cuba.

The Convertible Peso (*Peso Convertible*) is accepted everywhere without question. Most cash-machines issue only Convertible Pesos, as do the banks. Two warnings, however: be careful not to confuse the Convertible Cuban Peso (the word 'convertible' is clearly written on the front of the note) with the Cuban peso (*moneda nacional*) which is worth far less: the Convertible Peso is not exchangeable outside Cuba, so make sure you have none left in your wallet when getting onto the plane to fly back home.

In 1996, Cubans were allowed to hold US dollars for the first time. Many Cubans are desperate to earn their equivalent, the CUC, so that they can buy goods in shops such as clothes and shoes, and white goods such as washing machines that are only sold in CUC.

Outside the city centres, small goods such as chocolates or sandwiches are paid for in Cuban pesos. It is always useful to have a very small amount of pesos.

Exchange

It is best to arrive in Cuba with sterling (best) or euros, both in the form of cash and traveller's cheques. Changing US dollars in Cuba will incur a 10 per cent fee; sterling and euros do not. Remember that credit cards or traveller's cheques issued in the USA (mainly American Express) will not be accepted in Cuba.

Banks are usually open from 8am to 3pm, Monday to Friday. Exchange offices (*cadecas*) are open longer. Services include cashing traveller's cheques and withdrawing money over the counter using a credit or debit card.

Opening hours

Normal working hours on weekdays are 8am to 5.30pm. Banks generally are open from 8am to 3pm. Museums tend to open between 9am and 5pm Monday to Friday, and Sunday morning only. However, they have been known to close at unpredictable times, so it may be a good idea to phone ahead.

Police

Police officers in Cuba have a reputation for helpfulness and politeness, and rarely trouble foreigners. The main type of police are the PNR (Policía Nacional Revolucionaria), with light blue shirts and dark blue trousers. There are also tourist police who often speak English and who wear dark blue uniforms.

Post offices

The Cuban postal service is not the most reliable or the fastest, although it is comparable to other Latin American countries. Stamps (*sellos*) can be bought in hotels or post offices (*oficinas de correo*). The fastest way to send important letters or parcels is via international courier services such as DHL.

Public holidays

1 January Liberation Day. Anniversary of the Triumph of the Revolution.
1 May International Workers' Day.
25, 26 and 27 July Festivities in honour of the 26 July 1953 attack on Moncada Garrison.
10 October Beginning of the Wars of Independence.

Public transport

Getting around the island is relatively easy for foreigners and there are a number of options available. For those with limited time and more money, flying is the quickest way of covering the long distances on the island. There is a good network of internal flights, and flights can be booked at most travel agencies at reasonable cost.

For up-to-date details of long-distance bus, ferry and rail services consult the *Thomas Cook Overseas Timetable*, published six times a year. It is available to buy online at *www.thomascookpublishing.com* or from branches of Thomas Cook in the UK (*tel: 01733 416477*).

The next best option is long-distance buses. The best service is **Víazul**

A *camello* (camel bus) used by Cubans only

Telephone booths in Trinidad

(*www.viazul.cu*), although **Astro** also offers a reasonable service but with limited seats for foreigners. Coaches are relatively comfortable for long journeys and tend to be fairly punctual. They often have toilets and reclining seats, but the down side is that they often play low-quality videos and are often very cold due to the strong air-conditioning. Journeys are long, though; for example, Havana to Trinidad is a 5- or 6-hour journey.

Trains are best suited for people with time on their hands and limited budget. Breakdowns and long delays are commonplace, while the level of comfort and facilities are not high. The most popular route is between Havana and Santiago de Cuba, and tickets can be obtained from the Ferrotur offices in Havana.

Travelling by sea is also possible, the most used routes being between Havana and Isla de la Juventud.

In towns, public transport is available in the form of buses. Due to fuel shortages, long articulated lorries are used, called *camellos* (camels) due to their shape. Buses are very cheap but almost always crowded and uncomfortable, and not for tourists.

Sustainable tourism

Thomas Cook is a strong advocate of ethical and fairly traded tourism and believes that the travel experience should be as good for the places visited as it is for the people who visit them. That's why we firmly support The Travel Foundation: a charity that develops solutions to help improve and protect holiday destinations, their environment, traditions and culture. To find out what you can do to make a positive difference to the places you travel to and the people who live there, please visit *www.thetravelfoundation.org.uk*

Telephones

Run by ETECSA, the phone network is improving but is still not very efficient. New phones enable the use of pre-paid phone cards (*tarjetas telefónicas*), which can be bought at hotels, shops and ETECSA phone centres.

If you are calling Cuba, dial the international access code (e.g. *00* in the UK), then the country code for Cuba (*53*) followed by the local area code and phone number. The number of digits in local phone numbers varies according to the size of the town.

For private phones, international calls must be made through an operator and will always be reverse charge.

Phone codes in Cuba

From abroad: *00-53* – area code – number

From Cuba: *119* – country code – number

For direct dialling (*teleselección*): *0* – area code – number

These are the main regional codes.

All codes refer to provinces unless otherwise indicated.

Camagüey *32*
Cayo Largo *45*
Cienfuegos town *43*
Cienfuegos province *432*
Granma *23*
Guantánamo *21*
Havana city *7*
Holguín *24*
Isla de la Juventud *46*
Las Tunas *31*
Matanzas *45*
Pinar del Río province *82/85*
Pinar del Río town *48*
Sancti Spíritus *41*
Santiago de Cuba *22*
Trinidad town *419*
Varadero *45*
Villa Clara *42*
Zapata peninsula *45*
Directory enquiries *113*
Operator *00*
International operator for reverse charge calls *09*
To make a direct-dial international call from a public phone *119*, plus the international access code:
Australia *61*
Canada and USA *1*
New Zealand *64*
UK *44*

Time

Cuba is five hours behind GMT (Greenwich Mean Time), like the US east coast. In the summer there is daylight saving time, the same as in Europe.

Tipping

Tipping is recommended in hotels and restaurants, if only a small amount (a CUC or two for a US$25 meal). Cubans who work in the tourist industry tend to pool their tips to be shared between all staff. No tip is expected for food or accommodation at *casas particulares*, but musicians in bars or restaurants always expect to receive a donation for playing.

Toilets

Toilets are pretty basic, especially in public places, where they are often filthy. It is a good idea to carry toilet paper with you wherever you go, as it is generally not supplied. Wet wipes or antiseptic hand cream are also worth carrying.

In all places, toilet paper is placed in the rubbish bin rather than in the toilet, due to the poor state of the sewerage system.

Tourist information

Tourist information on Cuba can be found in the following countries.

Canada (Montreal)
440 Bd René Levesque Ouest, Suite 1105, H2Z 1V7, Montreal. Tel: 1-514-875-8004; fax: 1-514-875-8006; www.gocuba.ca

Canada (Toronto)
1200 Bay Street, Suite 305, M5R 2AS Toronto.
Tel: 1-866-404-2822; fax: 1-416-362-6799; www.gocuba.ca

United Kingdom
154 Shaftesbury Avenue (first floor), London, WC2H 8JT.

Tel: 44-20-7240-6655; tourism@cubasi.info

Within Cuba, there are tourist desks in most hotels, such as Rumbos, Horizontes or Cubanacán, which offer tours, transport or accommodation. In Havana, there is a small network of tourist information offices, called Infotur, which sell maps. Several can be found in Calle Obispo in Habana Vieja. The **Ministry of Tourism** is at *Calle 19 No 710, between Paseo and A, Vedado, Havana. Tel: 8334202.*

Useful information can also be obtained through these websites: *www.cubatravel.cu; www.infotur.cu; www.dtcuba.com* and *www.cubaweb.cu*

Travellers with disabilities

There are few facilities for people with disabilities. It is not easy to get around in towns, due to the high pavements and many potholes and loose paving stones. Some of the newer hotels in Varadero have some rooms adapted for wheelchair use, but most of the older hotels in Cuba, as well as *casas particulares*, have no facilities. It is recommended to do some research in advance and to book with a good tour company. One agency that caters for tourists with specific needs is **Cubanacán Turismo y Salud** (*www.cubanacan.cu*).

What to take

There are items that are in very short supply or unavailable in Cuba, which are advisable to take not only for your

Coco taxis waiting for passengers in Havana

personal use, but also for use as gifts.

In terms of what to wear, light and casual clothing is most suitable. As in other Latin countries, there is a clear distinction between male and female attire, and traditional attitudes prevail for the most part. A warm layer is useful, especially on long-distance buses where the air-conditioning is very strong. A waterproof is handy due to occasional tropical rainstorms.

Medicine is very expensive and scarce in Cuba, so bring all the medicines that you may need. Include items such as painkillers, indigestion pills, anti-diarrhoea preparations and rehydration salts, antibiotics and a first aid kit.

You should also bring items according to your individual circumstances such as insect repellent, razor blades, toilet paper, wetwipes, antiseptic hand-cream, condoms and other contraceptives, tampons,

disposable nappies, camera film and accessories, a torch and batteries, sun protection (high factor sun cream, glasses and a hat), and reading and writing materials.

Suitable gifts that will be gratefully received by Cubans include all of the above, as well as vitamin pills, soap, sewing needles, magazines and CDs or cassettes of western music (unavailable on the island). Some travellers take old clothes and shoes to wear while in Cuba, and donate them before returning home. Many Cubans cannot afford to buy new shoes or clothes, so any gifts (especially foreign goods) are welcomed.

However, it is advisable not to give gifts to locals or children in the street who ask for them, as this merely encourages further hassling of tourists. It is best to donate to Cubans whom you know or organisations that can distribute any gifts judiciously.

Index

Acknowledgements

Thomas Cook Publishing wishes to thank JOHN HARDEN for the photographs in this book, to whom the copyright belongs, except for the following images:

CLAIRE BOOBBYER 5, 18, 21, 27, 29, 32, 34, 37, 43, 50, 51, 124, 151, 153, 155, 156, 157, 162, 167, 174, 177, 179, 185, 186, 189
FLICKR/B.A.M 62, g magnan 104, lvroberts 106, jerroen 115, Mark Scott Johnson 121, boggin 143, Lauras512 161
PICTURES COLOUR LIBRARY 141, 164
WIKIMEDIA COMMONS/PHE James Schoole 134
WORLD PICTURES/PHOTOSHOT 110

The updater would like to thank Virgin Atlantic for help with the flight to Cuba.

For CAMBRIDGE PUBLISHING MANAGEMENT LTD:

Project editor: Rosalind Munro
Typesetter: Trevor Double
Proofreader: Eric Smith
Indexer: Karolin Thomas

SEND YOUR THOUGHTS TO
BOOKS@THOMASCOOK.COM

We're committed to providing the very best up-to-date information in our travel guides and constantly strive to make them as useful as they can be. You can help us to improve future editions by letting us have your feedback. If you've made a wonderful discovery on your travels that we don't already feature, if you'd like to inform us about recent changes to anything that we do include, or if you simply want to let us know your thoughts about this guidebook and how we can make it even better – we'd love to hear from you.

Send us ideas, discoveries and recommendations today and then look out for your valuable input in the next edition of this title.

Emails to the above address, or letters to Travellers Series Editor, Thomas Cook Publishing, PO Box 227, Unit 9, Coningsby Road, Peterborough PE3 8SB, UK.

Please don't forget to let us know which title your feedback refers to!